MW00928827

FROM STRESSED TO BEST

FROM STRESSED TO BEST

*A Proven Program
for Reducing Everyday Stress*

Ruth E Schneider and David S. Prudhomme

mederiwellness

MW Press, OH

First Edition -- 2014

ISBN: 978-1-304-42298-9

Published in the United States by: MW Press

mederiwellness

In Loving Memory

of

JULIE QUAYLE

A client who became a dear friend,
enthusiastic cheerleader
and valued mentor.

We miss you!

Table of Contents

Forward

<u>Testimonials:</u>

"*From Stressed To Best*™ takes MBTI® from theory to practice, and is a great tool for building effectiveness in individuals and teams, at work and at home. Seems everywhere I turn people are singing the praises of how *From Stressed To Best*™ is helping them, how much they got from both of you and how excited they are to learn more/do more … I'm excited and honored that I have had the opportunity to meet with you, learn your program, and bring it to my clients and company."

– Barb Miller, certified in MBTI® Step I™ & II™, certified in From Stressed to Best™, HR Manager/MBTI® Network Leader at P&G

"Our company invests heavily in training, and we look for return on that investment. The prevalent attitude was 'Oh boy, another training.' But the night after this training, I received four or five emails thanking me! With this training the return was immediate. Stress in the workplace is very much on an employer's mind. You can only stretch a rubber band so far. Ruth and David helped us understand how others on our team are wired. This is an incredible advantage."

-- Tom Mack, President, South Shore Marine, a US Top 100 boat dealership.

"I now understand my strengths and stressors and have an ability to shift out of stress in an instant, which allows me to be more productive with less stress. It has improved my communication with my loved ones, friends and even strangers because of my understanding of Personality Type. Life has become much easier, personally and professionally, since I have been exposed to the *From Stressed To Best*™ program…"

-- John Weir, Author and Sports Improvement Coach

"I had a patient yesterday that off handedly mentioned some stress and I had the time, so I had her do the short form assessment and reviewed her results with her…. It seemed to be life changing for her. I could literally see the light bulb in her head not only go off but explode in realization. There were many tears and much appreciation. I finally have something to offer besides yet more medicine!"

– Eric Van Fossen, PA-C, CH, certified in From Stressed to Best™

"I can't believe how much I learned about myself today. I had taken a personality test before at work and was not that impressed. What a difference David and Ruth make in understanding what it means and how I can actually use the information."

-- Judy Dushane, Accounts Receivable Representative

"I wanted to thank you both for this past Friday's session on personality style and stress management. I found it very informative and helpful. Having gone to a lot of professional development sessions during my 20+ years of teaching, I can say with certainty that this is by far the most beneficial session I have attended. I look forward to pursuing further the resources that were offered. So thanks again for providing such a great opportunity for the staff."

-- Brian, High School Teacher

"I have been the primary caretaker for my elderly father for years. My sister just left it all up to me and I resented it. Now I realize that I am perfectly suited to care for him and that she has none of the skills needed. Now I feel grateful for all of us that I am able to step up and take care of him. I can now look forward to my time with him again. I also now recognize that my sister does many other things I am not equipped to do."

-- JoAnn Dottore, Middle School Administrator

"I finished with a client today after several sessions using *From Stressed To Best*™. It was very moving. She's ESFJ with a mixed bag of S and N. She's a unique and complicated package to read without Step II. She was very grateful for the insight. As we looked at her facets it was predictable which ones stood out as being a part of some of her stress and past issues. Her "containment" facet was very emotional for her as well as her "accommodating" facet. She has an empty plate and doesn't know where to go with her life...kids are grown, divorced, ho hum job, living in the shadow on an ex. I've given her your card and asked that she follow up with you when she's ready. Amazing stuff; give yourselves a pat on the back......again!!!!

-- Douglas Van Fossen, D.O.,
certified in From Stressed to Best™

Preface

From Stressed To Best™, now a widely used program, was originally developed to help our clients at the Mederi Wellness Center.

Clients come to the Center for help with all types of issues – stop smoking, weight loss, fear, uneasiness, inability to focus, relationship issues, sports improvement and management of chronic pain, among others. Over time, it became evident to us that most of our clients were stressed – some were *very* stressed!   As we worked with them, it became obvious that if we could help them reduce their stress we could more efficiently and effectively help them with their other issues.

A history of practice with the 16 Personality Types made it clear that a one-size-fits-all approach to stress reduction just wouldn't work. We needed a new and different approach. A program to meld our knowledge of the conscious and subconscious mind with Personality Type and the latest research on stress. One that would address the different stressors of each of the 16 Personality types and incorporate tailored stress reduction strategies for each Type. And while the underlying science of such an approach is extensive, diverse and complex, it had to be easy to use and easily understood.

We began by using a self-assessment tool to provide us insight into the hard-wiring of each client's mind – what made them think, do and react as they did. We used this information to develop a tailored approach to stress reduction for them – and it worked! We were on a roll!

In the process of sharing the information we gleaned from their assessment with our clients, they were ecstatic to understand how their minds worked and why they found certain things stressful. They also began to gain an awareness of the other Personality Types and how their hard-wired differences could affect their interpersonal relationships. They were so enlightened and appreciative that they began referring our program to others. Some brought in their entire families. Local businesses and organizations were scheduling group sessions aimed at reducing stress from interpersonal relationships while team building.

The feedback was positive and reassuring! Clients were reporting remarkable stress reduction and improved relationships at home and at work. Some told us it changed their lives!

Although it didn't start as such, we now realized that our approach to reducing stress was perhaps revolutionary. We began documenting all aspects of our program and have published over 50 workbooks, practitioner guides and interpretive reports. We began teaching our program to other wellness practitioners and this has grown into our Certified Stress Reduction Specialist Program. **From Stressed To Best**™ is now being used by wellness professionals, trainers and businesses across the US and other countries around the world. One Fortune 50 corporation continues to expand the use of our products. It was time write this book!

This book is intended for use by anyone who is looking for self-help information to deal with their stress. It will also be of interest to parents, teachers, coaches, wellness professionals, team leaders and anyone else who has an interest in stress reduction.

It is our fervent hope that **From Stressed To Best**™ will play an important role in helping you and many others reduce your everyday stress and live a more satisfying and productive life.

Ruth E Schneider and David S Prudhomme

Introduction

Stress in our society is reaching epidemic proportions. Many people are searching for ways to reduce it and wellness professionals are looking for ways to help.

Unfortunately, a one-size-fits-all approach does not work! There are 16 individual, definable, well-recognized Personality Types which each need different approaches.

From Stressed To Best™ provides different stress reduction information and techniques for each of the 16 Types.

Using this book you will:

- ✓ Identify your individual inborn Personality Type – how your mind works.

- ✓ Understand what actually causes stress and why it differs by Personality Type.

- ✓ Learn how stress affects the human body.

- ✓ Learn how stress affects your mind – based upon your inborn hard-wiring.

- ✓ Learn what triggers your stress response, and why.

- ✓ Learn how to stretch beyond your natural reactions to avoid stress.

- ✓ Recognize the onset of your stress.

- ✓ Learn how to stop your stress response and harness the power of your natural relaxation response instead.

- ✓ Identify your inborn strengths, to help you achieve success in all aspects of your life.

- ✓ Understand why you think the way you do and why others don't think the way you wish they would.

- ✓ Understand other inborn Personality Types, to help you improve all your interpersonal relationships.

- ✓ Recognize stress in others and know how to best help people of various Personality Types return to balance.

You will find that the time you spend learning this program will have a rich, rewarding payback. You will be surprised how many things you will learn about yourself and others that you never realized before.

You will find:

- ✓ Your relationship with your spouse will improve.

- ✓ You will be better able to understand your children, your parents, and other family members.

- ✓ Your interactions will be more effective as you are better able to understand where your co-workers, friends, and acquaintances are coming from.

- ✓ You may even see your boss in a new light!

And people will notice a change in you, as well!

We have endeavored to keep the material practical and easy to use - a challenge, considering the diverse, in-depth bodies of technical knowledge upon which it is based. You will find you refer to it time and time again as one of your most powerful tools to help you improve your life and relationships.

Many people tell us it has changed their lives!

Chapter 1 – What is Stress?

If you ask what is the single most important key to longevity,
I would have to say it is avoiding worry, stress and tension.
George F. Burns

If we hear a nearby loud noise, our minds and bodies immediately switch to a "fight or flight" mode; we go on high alert! We stop, we look around, and we listen for any sign of impending danger. And until we reach the conclusion that there is no immediate danger, or that the danger has passed, we remain on high alert – ready to flee or take defensive action if need be.

This reaction is a familiar one – we've all experienced it. We didn't stop to think about what our reaction should be, it just happened! The reaction came from our subconscious mind and we responded in a spontaneous, pre-programmed and individual way.

Many things happen around us on a daily basis that pose no immediate danger; however, they often do create that same stress reaction. For example, a last-minute change in plans, a disagreement with a spouse or boss, a financial concern, an unruly child, a disagreement over how work should be accomplished, family interactions, conflicts in scheduling or a heavy schedule. Not to mention concerns about the economy, job security, or retirement. The list goes on and on.

Stress might be simply defined as a situation that causes a
negative, automatic mental and physical reaction.

How do we respond to such stress?

- ➢ Our bodies react similarly, but

- ➢ Our minds react differently based on our individual Personality Type.

Interestingly, our bodies react the same way whether we *actually* experience a stressful situation or we merely *think* about it.

THE PHYSICAL EFFECTS OF STRESS

Let's first address the physical reactions. All stress, whether experienced or imagined, triggers an immediate "Fight or Flight" response in the mind and body. "Fight or Flight" is an automatic survival mechanism that causes a cascade of adverse physiological changes to take place.

- ✓ Your adrenaline level goes up, causing a "gerbil wheel" of racing thoughts, reducing your ability to focus or concentrate. This can even affect your memory.
- ✓ Your Cortisol level goes up causing the body to stop burning fat.
- ✓ Your Blood pressure goes up and your heart rate increases.
- ✓ Your Blood sugar goes up.
- ✓ Your immune system is suppressed.
- ✓ Inflammation increases.
- ✓ Your hormones become unbalanced because the body is focused on producing "stress" hormones instead of the other important "feel good" hormones like oxytocin, serotonin, dopamine, and testosterone.
- ✓ Your digestion and metabolism are negatively impacted because the body is directing blood flow to your extremities to prepare to fight or run away.
- ✓ Your risk for heart attack, stroke, diabetes and even cancer all go up, especially when stress is on-going.
- ✓ Your chances for flare-ups from an autoimmune disease increase.
- ✓ You are more likely to experience depression or anxiety.
- ✓ The likelihood and frequency of headaches increases.
- ✓ Any pain is exacerbated.
- ✓ The symptoms of any chronic illness (Diabetes, Fibromyalgia, IBS, COPD, Hypertension, Arthritis, Cancer, Lupus, MS, etc.) are heightened.

Sometimes people have been stressed for so long that they don't even realize how stressed they actually are.

Chronic stress zaps energy
and adversely affects health and happiness.

They have come to accept this stress as "normal", or as a natural part of life. Because of this, they don't deal with their stress, it keeps building and they think of it as "normal." This is called the "Boiled Frog Syndrome."

Boiled Frog Syndrome

If you drop a frog into a pot of boiling water, it will jump out immediately.

If you put it into a pot of lukewarm water,
and turn the temperature up slowly,
it will not perceive the danger and will be boiled to death.

People who are chronically stressed may be suffering from this syndrome and not even know it. Do you, or others around you, have any of the following symptoms of Boiled Frog Syndrome?

✓ Do you get up in the morning and begin to rush around, thinking about all the things you need to accomplish and wondering how you will ever get it all done?

✓ Do you find that your temper is on a "hair trigger?"

✓ Do you wake up every day and go through the motions, feeling like you've lost your zest for life?

✓ Have you lost your patience with your spouse, your children, your parents, your co-workers or your boss?

✓ Do you daydream about escaping from your life and starting over?

✓ Do you feel your performance has slipped, or that things that used to be easy for you are now much more difficult?

✓ Do you wonder what happened to the loving person you married? He or she may have Boiled Frog Syndrome.

✓ Do you have a child, spouse, co-worker, parent or boss whose personality seems to have changed? He or she may be suffering from Boiled Frog Syndrome.

Change is everywhere and the speed of life has increased dramatically. Yet we still have the same need for rest, connection with others, recreation and time for ourselves.

If your life is overwhelming, hectic, or riddled with worry and frustration, you guessed it - you may be experiencing Boiled Frog Syndrome. Boiled Frog Syndrome is a sign of chronic stress. Chronic stress is now recognized by scientific and medical communities to be a major contributing factor to serious illness.

THE MENTAL EFFECTS OF STRESS

While the physical effects of stress are the same for everyone, the mental and emotional reactions to stress vary among individuals according to in-born differences in the hard-wiring of our individual brains.

We know that right or left-handedness is a hard-wired trait. We do not decide to prefer one hand over the other; the preference occurs naturally. If your primary hand is broken, you can get pretty good at using the other one. But chances are, when the cast comes off, you will revert back to using the one you naturally prefer.

Each individual's brain has other hard-wired preferences that determine what will cause them stress and how they will react to it. These inborn preferences follow each of us throughout our lives, just like handedness.

Imagine the tallest and fastest roller coaster in the world – some can't wait to ride it and view it as *fun*. Others are petrified and would not ride it *no matter what!* Still others could not bear to even *watch* others ride it!

Other people do not think and act like you do because they aren't hardwired the same way; their personalities are different. Personality differences shape our individual perspective, how we view the world, and how we react to the things happening around us. They also determine our reactions to stressful situations in our daily lives.

There are 16 different, definable and generally accepted Personality Types. Your personality can be characterized by one of them. The people around you can also be characterized by their individual Personality Types.

Understanding these in-born, fundamental differences in people is the foundation of this program. Realizing that individual differences are in-born, and knowing how to interact with the various Personality Types, is a key element for avoiding or reducing stress.

Identifying right or left-handedness is easy. Identifying Personality Type is a bit more involved. In this book you will learn your own Personality Type and how to reduce your stress. You will also learn how to recognize clues which can help you identify the different Personality Types of the people in your life. You will learn how to interact with each individual Personality Type more effectively. As you use this information on a daily basis, you will find that all your relationships will improve, both personal and professional. As your relationships improve, your stress will be reduced. Most people tell us that they wish they'd learned this information years ago. Many say they feel as though a heavy burden has been lifted from them and they have a new outlook on life.

Chapter 2 – What is Personality Type?

The shoe that fits one person pinches another;
there is no recipe for living that suits all cases. Carl Jung

Personality Type has long been touted in corporate circles for team building, communication improvement and leadership development. It can also be an important tool to help anyone understand themselves and others. This program teaches you how to use Personality Type to reduce your own stress and to understand how to be more effective in your life and relationships.

The basic concepts of Personality Type are based upon the work of pioneering psychiatrist Carl Jung. While working with his patients, he found they were often stuck in patterns of reaction that were not healthy for them and not serving them well. In 1921, he documented his observations of what he believed were in-born differences in a book titled "Psychological Types." Jung believed that by understanding their hard-wired preferences his patients would gain the ability to choose to act differently; to become more flexible and capable in more situations. In the 1940s, Katharine Cook Briggs and her daughter Isabel Briggs Myers also began thinking about inborn differences in people. They theorized that if women, who were entering the workforce in large numbers for the first time, were placed in jobs that matched their inborn preferences, they might be more comfortable entering the workforce. This mother-daughter team set about designing a set of questions that would help them determine the natural, hard-wired, personality preferences of these potential workers. Their instrument, the Myers-Briggs Type Indicator® (also referred to as the Myers-Briggs® or the MBTI®) has been refined and updated over the years and is the most researched and most validated personality tool in use in the world today. Each year some two million MBTI® assessments are administered world-wide.[1]

Many others have developed self-assessments to measure Personality Type; we have included ours in Chapter Two of this book. You will use this assessment to help you determine your Personality Type. Knowing your Personality Type is the key to using the From Stressed To Best™ program to manage your stress.

---

[1] Myers-Briggs Type Indicator® Step II™ (Form Q) Profile Copyright 2001, 2003 by Peter B. Myers and Katharine D. Myers. All rights reserved. Myers-Briggs Type Indicator, Myers-Briggs, MBTI, Step I, and Step II are trademarks or registered trademarks of the Myers & Briggs Foundation, Inc., in the United States and other countries.

AN OVERVIEW OF PERSONALITY TYPE

You may already be familiar with the concept of Personality Type; you may have even taken the MBTI®. Regardless of your experience level, it is important to begin by establishing a baseline understanding of Personality Type - the foundation upon which the *From Stressed To Best*™ program is based.

Do you know your Personality Type? Are you an "**ENTP**?" or maybe an "**ISFJ**?" or an "**ESFP**?" What do these letters tell you about yourself? Even if you already know your four letter Personality Type, please follow along and take our assessment.

Each Personality Type is designated by four letters. Each letter indicates one of four natural, hard-wired preferences. Again, these preferences are inborn - just like your natural preference to use your right or left hand for writing and other activities is inborn.

Each of these four preferences has two opposite poles. Each of us has a natural tendency to prefer to use one pole over the other. Each of these poles is assigned a letter. The four preferences are then put together to become the four-letter "Personality Type."

Here are all of the preferences and their letters at a glance:

1. Energy: The two ways people are energized.	**E** **Extraversion**	OR	**I** **Introversion**
2. Data-Gathering: The two ways people gather information.	**S** **Sensing**	OR	**N** **iNtuition**
3. Decision-Making: The two ways people make decisions.	**T** **Thinking**	OR	**F** **Feeling**
4. Prioritizing: The two ways people prioritize activities.	**J** **Judging**	OR	**P** **Perceiving**

The next four pages will help you understand the basis for Personality Type. As you read through them, you will begin to learn about your natural hard-wired preferences.

The self-assessment in Chapter Two uses more detailed questions to help you determine your Type.

ENERGY

The first letter of an individual's Personality Type is either **E** or **I**. This letter describes how a person directs and gathers energy.

This letter represents whether the person tends toward **_Extraversion_** (**E**) or **_Introversion_** (**I**).

- **_E - Extraverts_** direct their energy toward the outer world of people and activities. They get energy from interacting with others.

- **_I - Introverts_** direct their energy toward their inner world of thoughts, feelings, memories or ideas. They get energy from spending time alone, doing something they enjoy.

Extraverts and **Introverts** experience stress in different ways and they need to manage their energy differently.

- **_E – Extraverts_** tend to pull inward and become uncharacteristically quiet when they are stressed. They need to intersperse bursts of activity and conversation throughout the day to stay energized.

- **_I – Introverts_** tend to "lash out" or "freak out" when stressed. They need to intersperse periods of quiet time by themselves throughout the day to stay energized.

How do YOU manage your energy?

At this point,
which do you think you may be hard-wired to prefer?

Extraversion (E): ____

OR

Introversion (I): ____

DATA GATHERING

The second letter of an individual's Personality Type is either **S** or **N**. This letter describes how people take in data.

This letter represents whether the person tends to prefer *Sensing* (**S**) or *iNtuition* (**N**).

- **S - *Sensors*** prefer to begin with facts and details that can be perceived with the five senses.

- **N – *iNtuitives*** prefer to begin with the big picture - the ideas and connections that can be perceived by noticing patterns and nuances.

Sensors and **iNtuitives** are stressed by different situations and need to deal with stress in different ways.

- **S – *Sensors*** may be stressed by too much abstraction or things that don't seem to be practical. They need to get back to the facts to stay grounded.

- **N – *iNtuitives*** may be stressed by too many details or things that are very repetitive. They need to keep things in perspective.

How do YOU Gather Information?

At this point,
which do you think you may be hard-wired to prefer?

Sensing (S): ___

OR

Intuiting: (N): ___

DECISION MAKING

The third letter of an individual's Personality Type is either **T** or **F**. This letter describes how people make decisions.

This letter represents whether the person tends to lean toward making decisions using *Thinking* (**T**) or *Feeling* (**F**).

- *T - Thinking* Types tend to make decisions objectively and they focus on tasks.

- *F - Feeling* Types tend to decide subjectively and they focus on relationships.

Thinkers and **Feelers** are stressed by different situations and must learn to deal with stress in different ways.

- *T – Thinkers* may be stressed when decisions appear to be made inconsistently, or when they lack clear objective criteria. They need to understand the logic to stay grounded.

- *F – Feelers* may be stressed when decisions appear to be made without much regard for the people involved, or when they lack clear empathy. They need to understand the values used in making the decision to stay grounded.

How do YOU make Decisions?

At this point,
which do you think you may be hard-wired to prefer?:

Thinking (T): ____

OR

Feeling (F): ____

PRIORITIES

The fourth letter of an individual's Personality Type is either **J** or **P**. This letter describes how people prioritize the activities of their life.

This letter represents whether the person tends toward prioritizing as a *Judger* (J) or *Perceiver* (P).

- **J - Judgers** prefer prioritizing activities in order to accomplish the most, and do things most efficiently.

- **P - Perceivers** prefer prioritizing activities in order to experience things, to learn the most or follow what inspires them.

Judgers and **Perceivers** experience different types of pressure and must learn to deal with stress in different ways.

- **J – Judgers** may be stressed when their routines are interrupted, things do not go as planned or people around them are running late. They need to feel they are accomplishing things.

- **P – Perceivers** may be stressed by too much routine or a lack of flexibility. They need to feel inspired to accomplish things.

How do YOU prioritize?

At this point,
which do you think you may be hard-wired to prefer?:

Judging (J): ____

OR

Perceiving (P): ____

The various combinations of these four letters produce 16 different Personality Types. There are no "good" or "bad" Types. Each Personality Type has its own strengths as well as potential stressors.

We will examine each Personality Type in detail later, focusing on stress and how to deal with it.

USING PERSONALITY TYPE TO MANAGE STRESS

Each of the letters of a person's Personality Type has the potential for causing an "automatic" stress response in certain situations. For example:

- **E - Extraverts** – may be stressed by spending too much time alone doing paperwork.

- **I - Introverts** - may be stressed by spending too much time interacting with others.

- **S -Sensors** - may be stressed by listening to theories and "hair-brained" ideas.

- **N- iNtuitives** - may be stressed by having to pay attention to lots of details. .

- **T - Thinking** Types - may be stressed by people who seem emotionally "needy."

- **F - Feeling** Types - may be stressed by people who seem to "always be negative and critical."

- **J -Judgers** - may be stressed by disorganization and too many choices.

- **P - Perceivers** - may be stressed by too much structure and routine, or too many rules.

So, Personality Type not only identifies how individuals prefer to operate in the world, it also predicts which situations they will find to be most stressful. And, it also predicts how they will naturally react when under stress.

You have probably noticed that people react differently when they are under stress than when they are relaxed and feeling good. For example, some Personality Types may pine about the past, while others may worry about the future. Some become emotional and dramatic, while others become sullen and withdrawn.

> *The greatest weapon against stress is our ability to*
> *choose one thought over another.*
> *William James*

Here's a look at those reactions by preference:

- When **Extraverts** are stressed, they pull inward, becoming uncharacteristically quiet.

- When **Introverts** are stressed, they tend to become uncharacteristically vocal and "lash out" or "freak out".

- When **Sensors** are stressed, they are often overwhelmed by a big picture of doom and gloom. They see too much future and lose touch with the present moment.

- When **iNtuitives** are stressed, they become stuck on details and cannot see the big picture. They lose sight of the future and become mired in the failures of the past.

- When **Thinkers** are stressed, they experience hypersensitivity and are uncharacteristically emotional.

- When **Feelers** are stressed, they become overly critical and "dig in their heels," unable to see the options that will create harmony.

- When **Judgers** are stressed, they have difficulty making decisions, become forgetful or even lose things.

- When **Perceivers** are stressed, they make snap decisions or display compulsive behavior.

Each Personality Type has a predictable response to stress which causes an automatic shift to what we call their "Stress Mode." We will describe Stress Modes in detail later in this book as well as how to recognize and reverse your own automatic stress responses.

This book will show you how!

Let's get started by determining your Personality Type.

Chapter 3 – What Is Your Personality Type?

Nothing splendid has ever been achieved except by those
who dared believe that something inside them was
superior to circumstance. -- Bruce Barton

Your Personality Type is determined by your inborn, hard-wired preferences. Before moving on, let's identify *your* preferences!

There are a few things you need to know to be in the correct frame of mind for taking the self-assessment.

People do things for two different reasons – either it's a *natural* or in-born preference, or it's a *learned* behavior. You sometimes do things the way you *naturally* would do them and you sometimes do things the way you have *learned* to do them. The self-assessment is designed to help you identify how you *naturally* would do things.

Remember our earlier example: If you break your arm and it's the one you *naturally* prefer to use, you can get better at using your other one. But chances are, when the cast comes off, you will immediately go back to using the one you prefer *naturally*. Again, this self-assessment is designed to identify how you *naturally* would do things – how your brain is *naturally* "hard-wired".

The following self-assessment contains questions which ask you to choose between two answers. There are no "right" or "wrong" answers. As you now know, there are 16 different Personality Types and each one has its own strengths, potential stressors, and suggestions for dealing with stress. Answer the questions with the first answer that seems like you at your best, rather than spending time analyzing the questions. Your first reaction is the best answer!

To complete the self-assessment, put a checkmark next to the answer that seems most like you. Again, do not spend time analyzing the questions or your answers. Choose the first answer which seems like you when you feel most like yourself.

The assessment should take approximately 20 minutes. If you are having difficulty answering the questions for any reason, just stop for now, go do something else and then return to the assessment at a later time.

TURN THE PAGE TO BEGIN

When invited to a social function where I'm not likely to know anyone I usually:

Look forward to meeting lots of new people.	OR	Dread going and hope that I will find someone I know.	
Introduce myself to many people and talk easily with them. I enjoy small talk!	OR	Observe, listen and speak mostly when spoken to. I don't like small talk!	

My friends would tell you

I tend to usually say what's on my mind.	OR	I tend to share my thoughts only with a few carefully chosen people.	
I tend to be rather talkative.	OR	I'm known as a rather quiet person.	
People pretty much know about what's going on in my life.	OR	They often wonder what is going on in my head.	
I have lots and lots of friends. Everywhere we go, I'm bound to see somebody I know!	OR	I have a few very close friends and don't really feel the need to be that popular.	
The more friends, the better because I can always find someone to do something with!	OR	I mostly hang out with the same people and I like it that way. I don't need too many people in my life.	
I prefer to be around people most of the time rather than to be by myself too much.	OR	I enjoy spending a lot of time by myself -- reading, or writing or just thinking.	
I don't shy away from the spotlight; I can even be quite entertaining!	OR	I prefer to stay in the background and observe; I would not want to make a fool of myself.	
I might get loud and talk with my hands - especially if I'm excited about things!	OR	I tend to talk quietly and even laugh quietly so as not to draw too much attention to myself.	
I enjoy crowds and get energized by all the hustle and bustle!	OR	I prefer quiet places and quiet people; silence is good for my mood.	
I enjoy being up doing things rather than sitting around or doing paperwork!	OR	I enjoy working on something quietly and can easily do it for long periods of time.	

When learning to do something new

I prefer a "hands-on" approach – learning by doing.	OR	I prefer to watch someone else do something before I try doing it myself.	
I prefer face-to-face interaction so I can ask questions.	OR	I prefer to read ahead so I can think about things before having to do them and figure out if I still have questions before I watch a demonstration.	

When I want to express my thoughts or opinions

I prefer to talk them over with someone – it seems to help me clarify my thoughts.	OR	I prefer to think or even write about what I would like to say and how I would like to say it.	
I enjoy getting up in front of people and extemporaneously talking about my views.	OR	I enjoy writing about my views and saying things exactly the way I want to say them.	

When I listen to what people are saying

I tend to tend to like them to be specific and keep things simple.	OR	I enjoy the intellectual stimulation of figuring something out.	
I like them to give me the facts and details up-front to help me understand.		I like to know the purpose of what they are telling me so I can put it into context before hearing the details.	
I tend to think about whether or not they seem to be realistic.	OR	I am interested if they seem to be interesting, unique and imaginative.	
I prefer listening to someone who has a common sense approach.	OR	I like listening to someone who has new ideas.	
I like to hear all the details and go along for the ride.	OR	I like to know the big picture before I hear too many details.	
I like to visualize all the details as they talk.	OR	I like to think about how what they are saying relates to other things I know.	

When I do something:

I want to know the proper way of doing it. And, I like doing things again and again so I can perfect them.	OR	I tend to get bored if I have to do the same thing in the same way over and over again; I like to experiment with new ways of doing something.	
Once I begin, I usually focus on the details needed to complete a job.	OR	After working for a while, I realize I need to pull myself back from all the interesting tangents I've followed.	
I want to know the practical use. I don't like to waste time on things I don't absolutely need to know.	OR	I sometimes find that ideas are interesting even if I'm not sure exactly how they could be used.	
I tend to rely on my past experience to guide me.	OR	I tend to rely on my knowledge of how things work to guide me.	
If I (or someone I know) has done something before, that gives me a pretty good idea of how it will turn out next time.	OR	I tend to believe that experience is only one factor and doesn't necessarily predict how things will turn out.	
I like doing something that feels comfortable. I have a favorite restaurant and a dish I am very likely to order when I go there. I like knowing I can depend on it to be exactly the way I like it.	OR	I like to experiment with things that I haven't done before. I like to try new restaurants and I like to try foods that I haven't tried before to see what they are like.	
I can be counted upon to hold up family traditions. I enjoy the feeling of ritual and the dependability of events done in traditional ways.	OR	I can be counted upon to take a unique approach, collect or wear unique items, or think of unusual ways to celebrate traditional events.	
I like to do it the way others do.	OR	I really like to do it my way.	
I like to start with the facts and then I can more easily understand the theory behind the facts.	OR	I like to start with the theory and then I can more easily remember the details about specific examples.	
I find I get pleasure from knowing I can do something well.	OR	I find I get pleasure from finding a new way to do something.	
I like using checklists and procedures because they help me do things right.	OR	I dislike having to follow a checklist or a procedure because it hinders my creativity.	

Whenever I face a problem:

	OR		
I pride myself on my ability to look at it objectively.	OR	I need to understand how everyone involved feels about it.	
I tend to make a list of pros and cons or use some type of analytical tool to better understand the situation.	OR	I tend to study the situation and the people involved to be sure I understand everything that is going on with each of them.	
I try to stay as objective as possible so that I make a good decision.	OR	I try to stay compassionate as possible so that I am fair with everyone.	
I can usually figure out the correct solution right away as long as I have all the facts.	OR	I hesitate when choosing a solution sometimes because I do not want to hurt people.	
I like to get it out in the open and deal with it.	OR	I often go along with others just to get the problem behind us.	
I want to be sure all my questions are answered before moving on.	OR	I believe questions will be answered in time so I usually wait and see.	
Other people sometimes think I am confrontational.	OR	Other people sometimes wonder what I really think about the situation.	
I want to understand everything that is wrong.	OR	I like to focus on what is working so we can build on that.	
I want to convince people to adopt my solution once I have things figured out.	OR	I want to get everybody on the same page so I continue to look for other alternatives even after I think I know what is best.	
I get upset if I can't do what seems right because others won't agree.	OR	I like to support what the majority of people want to do.	
I tend to easily notice what is wrong.	OR	I tend to easily notice what is right.	

When working with others:

	OR		
I just expect them to do whatever it takes to get the job done; that's what they are here to do.	OR	I am appreciative of the work people do to get the job done; I enjoy it when everyone is happy and productive.	
I sometimes have to make tough decisions and so I just do it.	OR	I work very hard to get people to agree and go along with a decision especially if it is unpopular.	
I focus on the problem and the solution; I am not here to win a popularity contest.	OR	I like to use gentleness and affection to get people on board with a solution.	
I will point out mistakes so that people don't make the same mistake twice.	OR	I will point out a mistake when it is important enough and I will also point out what they do well to balance my comments.	
I like working with people who like to discuss the project and even argue about which approach might be best.	OR	I like working with people who get along together well and don't have too many questions.	
I am sometimes seen as confrontational.	OR	I am sometimes seen as deferential.	
I am frustrated when people want to revisit decisions we have already made.	OR	I am frustrated when people want to implement decisions without taking all the impacts into consideration.	

My best days are the ones:

		OR		
	When I know what I am going to do and then I am able to do it without any interruptions.	OR	Something interesting comes up and I am able to drop everything and just go do it.	
	When I have prepared thoroughly and things go smoothly.	OR	Everything just seems to come together.	
	When my time is used wisely and I get things done in the time I allotted to them.	OR	I enjoy my day and I learn something new and unexpected.	
	I am able to complete a project.	OR	When I have something interesting to do.	
	When I am busy and getting things done.	OR	When I end up learning something unexpected.	
	When I can work on one thing at a time.	OR	When I can pick and choose what I work on depending on my mood.	
	When I feel organized and efficient.	OR	When I feel inspired and energized.	
	When my well-deserved, well-planned vacation goes just the way I planned it.	OR	When I discover something new and unexpected and do it instead of what I thought I was going to do for vacation.	
	When I am in my routine and have my rhythm.	OR	When I am in the mood and everything is flowing.	

When I work on a project:

		OR		
	I like to plan it out ahead of time so that I know what needs to be done and how much time it will take me to complete it.	OR	I like to start it and see where it takes me – it is exciting to discover more as I move along.	
	I like to follow procedures that have worked before.	OR	I like to change things up and try new ways of doing things.	
	I tend to organize it so it flows well and will be done on time.	OR	I tend to get bored easily and move on to newer, more interesting projects.	
	I tend to finish whatever I start.	OR	I tend to have many unfinished projects.	
	I like to get started and finish early.	OR	I like to do things at the last minute.	
	I tend to become stressed if something goes wrong.	OR	I tend to be good at figuring out why something went wrong and fixing it on the fly.	
	I tend to become stressed if there are too many changes after I've already started.	OR	I tend to get energized if I see a new approach as I work and am comfortable changing things as I go along.	
	I like to color-code things and keep track of my progress.	OR	I like to spend my time figuring things out as I go rather than doing a bunch of planning and record keeping.	
	I like to feel I am well-prepared.	OR	I like to do things off the cuff.	
	I tend to work at a steady pace from beginning to end.	OR	I tend to work in bursts and spurts when I am inspired.	

TURN THE PAGE TO SCORE YOUR RESULTS

QUICK SELF-ASSESSMENT OF PERSONALITY TYPE – SCORING SHEET

Your page 1 Results indicate whether you prefer **Extraversion (E)** or **Introversion (I)**

Number of checkmarks on Left side of Page 1:	Number of checkmarks on Right side of Page 1:

- If your Left side number is higher, you are likely Extraverted so enter an E in the first space at the bottom of the page.
- If your Right side number is higher, you are likely Introverted so enter I in the first space at the bottom of the page.
- If your Left and Right side numbers are equal, you are likely Introverted so enter an I in the first space at the bottom of the page.

Your page 2 Results indicate whether you prefer **Sensing (S)** or **iNtuition (N)**

Number of checkmarks on Left side of Page 2:	Number of checkmarks on Right side of Page 2:

- If your Left side number is higher you are likely Sensor so enter an S in the second space at the bottom of the page.
- If your Right side number is higher, you are likely iNtuitive so enter an N in the second space at the bottom of the page.
- If your Left and Right side numbers are equal, you are likely iNtuitive so enter an N in the second space at the bottom of the page.

Your page 3 Results indicate whether you prefer **Thinking (T)** or **Feeling (F)**

Number of checkmarks on Left side of Page 3:	Number of checkmarks on Right side of Page 3:

- If your Left side number is higher, you likely prefer Thinking so enter T in the third space at the bottom of the page.
- If your Right side number is higher, you likely prefer Feeling so enter F in the third space at the bottom of the page.
- If your Left and Right side numbers are equal, and you are male, you likely prefer Feeling so enter F in the third space at the bottom of the page.
- If your Left and Right side numbers are equal, and you are female, you likely prefer Thinking so enter T in the third space at the bottom of the page.

Your page 4 Results indicate whether you prefer **Judging (J)** or **Perceiving (P)**

Number of checkmarks on Left side of Page 4:	Number of checkmarks on Right side of Page 4:

- If your Left side number is higher you are likely judging so enter a J in the last space at the bottom of the page.
- If your Right side number is higher, you are likely Perceiving so enter P in the last space at the bottom of the page.
- If your Left and Right side numbers are equal, you are likely Perceiving so enter P in the last space at the bottom of the page.

For Stress Reduction Guides, Workbooks and other products visit
www.StressedToBest.com

Now that you know the four letters of your Personality Type, you can begin to explore the many ways in which you can use this information.

First we will examine each letter of your Personality Type so that you will understand its impact upon every aspect of your life, both personal and professional.

Then we will put all the letters together and show you how the combination of letters creates your Personality Type.

Finally, we will show you how to use the combined four letters of your Personality Type to recognize when you are stressed, and to understand how to manage and remove the stress.

As you work through the program, you will also learn a great deal about the Personality Types you interact with on a daily basis. You will come to a better understanding of why others act and react the way they do. This will have a powerful impact on your ability to improve all of your relationships.

Sometimes people feel that the self-assessment reached the wrong conclusion. This occasionally happens for one of several reasons.

➢ The person feels they have some characteristics of each of the two letters. In fact, people often have answers on each side of the page. So if you think you have a mixture, your probably do. That is not a problem. You will be able to determine the Personality Type that is the best fit for you as you work through this book.

➢ The person has always believed they are one or the other. Just because you've always thought of yourself as *Extraverted*, for example, doesn't make it so. *Introverts* with certain *Extraverted* qualities may grow up believing they are actually *Extraverted* and vice versa. And, the definitions may not be what you thought they were! For example, *Extraversion* is not just about being "talkative" and Introversion does not mean "shy."

➢ Sometimes people take the self-assessment while under stress and this can affect their responses. We will cover this extensively later in the book.

Keep in mind that YOU answered the questions!
YOU ARE THE EXPERT ON YOU!

This book will guide you toward a better understanding
of your Personality Type so that
you will be able to fully benefit from the program.

Chapter 4 – How You Manage Your Energy

When people are tired, they are stressed more easily.
Managing your energy level pays big dividends.

The first letter of your Personality Type is either **E** – which stands for **Extravert** or **I** – which stands for **Introvert**. This letter describes how you manage your energy. It indicates where you get your energy from and what you direct your energy toward.

WHY MANAGING YOUR ENERGY IS IMPORTANT

Are you tired or even exhausted? Many people tell us they are.

A major contributor to that common condition is not understanding how to manage your energy. If you never plug in your cell phone, the battery will drain; if you don't manage your energy, <u>your</u> battery will drain.

Good news! We've found some things that work, depending on whether you are **E or I.**

E - Extraverts and I – Introverts:

- ✓ Are energized by different things.

- ✓ Are worn down by different things.

- ✓ Need to use different techniques to stay feeling and performing at their best.

ENERGY ISSUES ARISE WHEN:

People do not know how to manage their energy
OR
They do not take the time to do what is necessary to have enough energy to manage their stress.

ARE YOU EXTRAVERTED OR INTROVERTED?

*Approximately 75% of people are **Extraverted***
*Approximately 25% are **Introverted***

The following Table illustrates the differences in energy between **Extraverts** and **Introverts**.

TABLE: E AND I ENERGY DIFFERENCES

EXTRAVERTS (E):	How they differ.	INTROVERTS (I):
Engaging with people by talking, playing sports, or performing for an audience.	What energizes them?	Spending time thinking, reminiscing, tinkering or working independently.
Outward toward people and things — getting and giving energy when around people and participating in activities.	Where do they direct their energy?	Inward toward their own inner world of thoughts, feelings, memories and ideas.
Sitting quietly for long periods of time reading, writing or doing computer work or paperwork.	What drains their energy?	Interacting with the outer world, talking and participating in group activities for long periods of time.
Breaking up time spent doing paperwork and quiet tasks into smaller blocks of time. Developing a rhythm of working for 20-30 minutes and then getting up to talk to someone or do something active.	What strategies help them manage their energy?	Getting by themselves before and after periods of activity or being with other people. Resting after a busy day to recharge and be ready to go out and socialize.
Periodically engaging in activities with other people.	How they recharge their batteries	Periodically spending time by themselves engaging in an activity they enjoy such as reading, writing or tinkering.

As you can see, **Extraverts** and **Introverts** naturally prefer to interact with people differently. Of course we all sometimes interact with others and we all sometimes work quietly in our heads. The most important thing to understand about yourself at this point is how to best manage your energy so you stay well-rested and ready to go.

MANAGING YOUR ENERGY:

We all deal more effectively with every situation when we have the energy to do so. That's just common sense. But do you know how to manage yourself in a way that ensures you indeed have the energy to be most effective?

Learning to manage your energy is a simple yet powerful concept that begins with understanding the first letter of your Personality Type. Understanding this concept will make a tremendous difference in your life!

If you get tired of everything in life, learn to rest, not to quit.

-- Unknown

HOW EXTRAVERTS NEED TO MANAGE THEIR ENERGY:

Extraverts often push through to complete things without taking breaks believing they should be able to just keep on working. But, pushing through just continues to wear them out and actually lowers their productivity.

It is important for *Extraverts* to realize that they get energy from interacting with people and things in their environment. Going for a quick walk, or taking a short break to talk on the phone or visit someone will reenergize them and put them back in high gear.

We find that when *Extraverts* understand this about themselves and develop a rhythm of taking short breaks, they report far more overall energy. Again, a simple solution that yields big results!

> *For Extraverts:*
> *Recharge with activity and by interacting with others.*

If you need to do homework, paperwork, or computer work here are some tips:

1. *Extraverts* work best when there is activity around them rather than sitting quietly by themselves. Try having *Extraverted* children do homework at the kitchen table while you are cooking dinner. Engage them periodically by asking them to tell you what they're working on. The interaction will keep them energized. Teaching them to work this way will be a lifelong help to them.

2. If you are an *Extravert* and have paperwork or computer work to do, turn on the TV, work in a room with other people, or listen to music while you work. Take a break as soon as your energy wanes. Go talk to someone or go for a brisk walk, and then come right back to the paperwork. You will be amazed at how much more productive you can be.

HOW INTROVERTS NEED TO MANAGE THEIR ENERGY:

Introverts often run themselves ragged, especially because this is an **Extraverted** world! Remember that approximately 75% of people are **Extraverts. Introverts** often feel they lack the energy to keep up, but they try! They run from activity to activity and they end up exhausted at the end of the day.

It is important for **Introverts** to understand that *they require quiet time alone, every single day.* They need to spend time independently doing something they *enjoy,* in order to recharge their batteries. It is not a luxury; it is essential for their well-being.

We find that most **Introverts** are relieved when they understand that this is how they are designed. When they allow themselves the time and space to rest and relax, without guilt, they report feeling much more energized. How simple is that?

For Introverts:

Recharge with quiet time every single day

to focus inside your head - shutting off the outer world for a time.

It is not a luxury; it is essential to your well-being!

If you need to participate in a group activity, attend a social function, go on a job interview or make a presentation here are a few tips:

1. Be sure you are rested before you go. Take the time to do something by yourself that you enjoy doing. Know that this time is not being wasted; it is preparing you for the important event. Your cellphone won't last very long if it has been used day after day and never charged. You need to charge your own batteries too!

2. Schedule your day with "down time" throughout. Take a 15 minute break mid-morning and get away from the hustle and bustle. Have lunch on your own, away from your desk, or with one of your close, quiet friends. Schedule time to regroup between meetings or appointments. Take advantage of waiting time by always having a book or magazine handy that interests you. Whenever there is a lull in activity, pull it out and recharge by shutting out the outside world for a moment or two.

EXTRAVERTS AND INTROVERTS UNDER STRESS

Stress changes a person's energy.

➢ **Extraverts** who are stressed tend to pull inward and become uncharacteristically quiet. A person who is sullen and detached, might be an **Extravert** who is stressed!

➢ **Introverts** who are stressed tend to "lash out" or "freak out." A person who is animated and speaking out may be an **Introvert** experiencing stress.

Remember:
To return to balance when stressed,
You must return to your natural state of energy.

STRESS IN EXTRAVERTS (E):

Extraverts tend to withdraw and become quiet when stressed rather than being energetic, outgoing and talkative like they usually are. This change in energy is a visible sign of stress, once you know to look for it.

✓ They pull inward and lose their desire to engage with people.

✓ They no longer want to participate in the activities they usually like.

When **Extraverts** are stressed they might want to be by themselves all day, but that will not help them return to balance.

Recharging their batteries by getting out and doing something or interacting with others is the best way for an **Extravert** to beat stress!

To manage stress most effectively **Extraverts** need to get out and reconnect with people, doing something active and social that they enjoy.

Introverts might fail to notice that this energy change in an **Extravert** is a sign of stress. To the **Introvert**, the lower level of energy may be a welcome respite in the relationship! Or, they might even think of it as the other person returning to "normal." They are sometimes caught off-guard when they discover that the **Extravert** is stressed over a problem in their relationship.

STRESS IN INTROVERTS (I):

Introverts tend to become animated and vocal when they are stressed rather than quiet and calm as they usually are. This change in energy is a visible sign of stress, once you know to look for it.

- ✓ They lash out at the people closest to them, like a pressure cooker that has finally reached the boiling point.

- ✓ They say the first thing that comes into their mind, rather than thinking things through like they normally do.

When **Introverts** are stressed they might want to pick a fight, but this is not productive and will not help them return to balance. Recharging their batteries by stepping away from everyone and doing something they enjoy is the best way for **Introverts** to beat stress!

To deal with stress most effectively, Introverts need to step away from the fray and get by themselves. Once alone they will be able to calm themselves and return to balance.

Again, stress in **Introverts** is exacerbated by the fact that most people are **Extraverted**. **Introverts** have to summon the energy to deal with people all day long. Even interacting with other **Introverts** takes energy!

Interestingly, the high energy levels of an **Extravert** can trigger stress in an Introvert, especially when they are already tired or stressed. The **Extravert** is not behaving any differently; the Introvert is just unable to sum up the energy to meet the **Extravert's** energy level at the time. When the **Introvert** finally shows that stress by talking, the **Extravert** might believe they are just having a conversation. The **Extravert** may not recognize this behavior as stress because it seems "normal" to them and they are glad to finally be getting a response and having a conversation! But, when Introverts are stressed, you do not want to listen to what they are saying because their verbiage is only a sign of stress, not a reflection of how they think or what they really want to say.

Leave an extravert alone for two minutes and he will reach for his cell phone. In contrast, after an hour or two of being socially "on," we introverts need to turn off and recharge. My own formula is roughly two hours alone for every hour of socializing.
— Jonathan Rauch

USING KNOWLEDGE OF E AND I TO GET ALONG WITH OTHERS

As you begin to understand your energy, you will be less stressed.

As you begin to understand others' energy, your relationships will improve.

E and I EXAMPLE

Clara and her son Brian are both Extraverted. Brian married Tiffany -- who is Introverted.

Clara wanted to make her daughter-in-law feel at home, so she worked very hard to be sure Tiffany didn't feel left out of the family conversations. She made sure to ask Tiffany for her opinion on everything that was discussed.

Tiffany, however, felt awkward and told Brian she felt like his mother was putting her under the microscope! Brain told her, "That's ridiculous. She likes you!" Nonetheless, Tiffany began dreading the family functions.

When Clara learned that Tiffany was Introverted, she stopped trying to get her to talk. Tiffany relaxed and began enjoying being with the family by observing them and how they interacted with each other. And, to Clara's surprise, Tiffany actually did chime in occasionally, once she was comfortable. Mission accomplished!

Understanding and managing Energy is important! Now you have the tools you need to put it into action to improve your life.

Communication and relationship problems
are often complicated and compounded
by energy issues.

ARE YOU STILL UNSURE IF YOU ARE E OR I?

Hopefully the preceding pages have helped you clarify your inborn preference for *Extraversion* or *Introversion*. If you still need help deciding, consider the following:

✓ Sometimes a person will say, "I think I used to be an *Extravert* but now I seem to be more of an *Introvert*." In fact, now you know that this might be a sign of chronic stress.

✓ How do you best charge your batteries? Remember:

- *Es* charge their batteries by interacting with people.

- *Is* charge their batteries with "down time" by themselves.

✓ How do you behave when stressed?

- *Es* withdraw and get uncharacteristically quiet.

- *Is* become uncharacteristically vocal and animated.

Remember, you answered the questions in the first place; you are the expert on you! You are in the best position to determine whether you are *Extraverted* or *Introverted*. The self-assessment is just a tool used to help you decide; you know best.

If you are still undecided, don't be concerned. It will become clear as you proceed through the rest of the book!

Knowing how to stay energized
is an important strategy for reducing stress.

Now you understand *Extraversion* and *Introversion*. You now also realize that this element of Personality Type determines how a person must effectively manage their energy.

The concepts of *Extraversion* and *Introversion* are important to understanding your Modes of Operating. Next, we'll address these Modes of Operating – how people gather information and how they make decisions

Chapter 5 – Modes of Operating

Always be yourself, express yourself, have faith in yourself, do not go out and look for a successful personality and duplicate it.
Bruce Lee

Before we get into the details of the second and third letters of your Personality Type, let's first look at how those two letters are related.

Either the second or third letter of your Personality Type is your Best Mode of Operating. The other one is your Secondary Mode of Operating. These Modes are distinct, every day, hard-wired mental activities based upon your Personality Type.

Your second letter is either S or N. It will be S if you naturally prefer gathering information starting with the details. It will be N if you naturally begin with the big picture. We all gather information in both ways, but have a preference to begin with one or the other.

Your third letter is either T or F. It will be T if you naturally prefer objective analysis for decision making. It will be F if you rely mostly on subjective analysis for decision making. Again, you are hard-wired to pay more attention to one over the other.

WHY IS IT IMPORTANT TO UNDERSTAND MODES OF OPERATING?

Your mind is capable of using *both* ways of *Gathering Information*. And you *do* use both ways! You look at the facts and details using **Sensing,** and you put things into perspective using *iNtuition*. Because you rely on one more than the other, it is more developed and you are more capable when using it.

Likewise you are capable of looking at decisions from *both* the perspective of **Thinking** and **Feeling**, and you often do. You use **Thinking** to consider the pros and cons and to analyze data, and you use **Feeling** to consider your values and the impact a decision might have on others. Again, one tends to be more developed but you do use both.

Again, everyone uses all four Modes of Operating – we Gather Information using both **Sensing** and *iNtuition* even though we rely on one more than the other. And, we Make Decisions using both **Thinking** and **Feeling** even though we do tend to naturally prefer one. *All four Modes of Operating are used in every single Personality Type* - some are just more developed! The *order* of development of these hard-wired preferences differ based upon Personality Type.

Understanding the order of your preferences for all four of these Modes of Operating (*Sensing*, *iNtuition*, *Thinking* and *Feeling*) is the cornerstone of the *From Stressed to Best*™ program. Each Personality Type has a BEST Mode of operating, a secondary mode of operating, a third mode and a Stress Mode of operating.

Here is how that works.

BEST Mode of Operating:

Your BEST mode is your strongest, most developed Mode of Operating. It is what your brain is hard-wired to do best. You might be best at one of the DATA GATHERING Modes (S or N) or you might be best at one of the DECISION MAKING Modes (T or F). It depends upon your four letter Personality Type. This means your Best Mode of operating will be either the second letter or the third letter of your Personality Type. You will know which one is your Best Mode of Operating in a few more pages!

Almost every wise saying has an opposite one,
no less wise, to balance it.
George Santayana

NATURAL BALANCE: The SECONDARY Mode of Operating:

Your Secondary Mode is the second most developed of your Modes of Operating. It supports you by *balancing* your BEST Mode in two important ways.

1. **OPPOSITE MODE OF OPERATING**:
   If your BEST mode is a DATA GATHERING Mode (S or N) then your Secondary Mode will be a DECISION MAKING Mode (T or F) because you need the ability to both GATHER INFORMATION and to MAKE DECISIONS!

   Likewise, if your Best Mode is a DECISION MAKING Mode (T or F), then your Secondary Mode will be a DATA GATHERING Mode (S or N).

2. **OPPOSITE ENERGY**:
   If you are an *Extravert*, your BEST Mode is *Extraverted* and your Secondary Mode helps balance you by being *Introverted*. This Secondary Mode allows you to work quietly inside your head when required.

   Likewise, if you are *Introverted*, your BEST Mode is *Introverted* and your Secondary Mode is *Extraverted*. This Secondary Mode allows you to interact with the people around you when required.

THIRD Mode of Operating:

Your Third Mode of operating is less developed than both your Best Mode and your Secondary Mode, but is still available for your use. You have to spend more conscious effort to use this Mode of Operating. It is like writing with your non-preferred hand – it can be done but requires more concentration.

STRESS Modes of Operating:

Your Fourth Mode of operating is your least developed, and least effective Mode of Operating. When you are stressed, your brain "shuts down" and switches to its least effective Mode of operating. Not the best way to solve a problem, as you can imagine! We call this least effective mode of operating your STRESS Mode. Your Stress Mode is the opposite of your Best Mode.

1. OPPOSITE ENERGY:
   If you are *Extraverted*, your STRESS Mode is *Introverted*. You will remember from the last chapter that *Extraverts* tend to withdraw when they are stressed. This is not the most effective way for *Extraverts* to solve their problems.

   If you are *Introverted*, your STRESS Mode is *Extraverted*. Again you will recall from the last Chapter that *Introverts* who are stressed tend to lash out or "freak out." Again, this is not the best way for *Introverts* to solve their problems.

2. OPPOSITE PREFERENCE:
   If your Best Mode is Gathering Information using *S -Sensing*, your Stress Mode will be the opposite of *S* which is N - *iNtuition*. Likewise if your Best Mode is *N*, your Stress Mode will be *S*.

   If your Best Mode is Making Decisions using *T – Thinking*, your Stress Mode will be the opposite preference which is *F – Feeling*. Likewise if your Best Mode is *F*, your Stress Mode will be *T*.

You will learn how to switch from your Stress Mode to your Best Mode as you continue to work through this book.

Once you replace negative thoughts with positive ones,
you'll start having positive results.
Willie Nelson

For now, here is a chart you can use to identify your Modes of Operating.

TYPE	BEST Mode	Secondary Mode	Third Mode	STRESS Mode
ESTP	Extraverted Sensing	Introverted Thinking	Extraverted Feeling	Introverted iNtuition
ESFP	Extraverted Sensing	Introverted Feeling	Extraverted Thinking	Introverted iNtuition
ESTJ	Extraverted Thinking	Introverted Sensing	Extraverted iNtuition	Introverted Feeling
ENTJ	Extraverted Thinking	Introverted iNtuition	Extraverted Sensing	Introverted Feeling
ENFP	Extraverted iNtuition	Introverted Feeling	Extraverted Thinking	Introverted Sensing
ENTP	Extraverted iNtuition	Introverted Thinking	Extraverted Feeling	Introverted Sensing
ENFJ	Extraverted Feeling	Introverted iNtuition	Extraverted Sensing	Introverted Thinking
ESFJ	Extraverted Feeling	Introverted Sensing	Extraverted iNtuition	Introverted Thinking
ISTP	Introverted Thinking	Extraverted Sensing	Introverted iNtuition	Extraverted Feeling
ISFP	Introverted Feeling	Extraverted Sensing	Introverted iNtuition	Extraverted Thinking
ISTJ	Introverted Sensing	Extraverted Thinking	Introverted Feeling	Extraverted iNtuition
INTJ	Introverted iNtuition	Extraverted Thinking	Introverted Feeling	Extraverted Sensing
INFP	Introverted Feeling	Extraverted iNtuition	Introverted Sensing	Extraverted Thinking
INTP	Introverted Thinking	Extraverted iNtuition	Introverted Sensing	Extraverted Feeling
INFJ	Introverted iNtuition	Extraverted Feeling	Introverted Thinking	Extraverted Sensing
ISFJ	Introverted Sensing	Extraverted Feeling	Introverted Thinking	Extraverted iNtuition

Now let's take an in-depth look at the second letter of Personality Type – The Mode of Operating you use to Gather Information!

Chapter 6 – Your Data Gathering Mode of Operating

Much of the stress in any relationship comes from misunderstanding or misinterpreting what is said. Understanding how people gather information can help avoid these conflicts.

The second letter of your Personality Type describes the Mode of Operating you use to gather information. This affects the way you perceive everything around you.

If you ever doubt your ability to communicate effectively, or if you conclude that others "just don't get it," maybe it is a matter of the hard-wired differences between *S* and *N*.

WHY UNDERSTANDING YOUR DATA GATHERING MODE IS IMPORTANT

Understanding this concept will change the way you communicate and the way you listen to others. Why?

Because *Sensors* and *iNtuitives* look at things from different perspectives, they listen differently and they communicate differently.

Everyone uses both of these ways of gathering information, but one of the two describes what you tend to notice first, as well as how you prefer to communicate about the information you most naturally notice.

S – Sensors and N – iNtuitives:

- ✓ Pay attention to different types of information.
- ✓ Communicate information differently
- ✓ Evaluate credibility differently.

> Communication issues often arise when we see a situation from different angles and we cannot understand where the other person is coming from! Or, when we fail to provide the appropriate context or level of detail to successfully explain what we see to others.

DO YOU PRIMARILY USE SENSING (S) OR INTUITION (N)?

*Approximately 75% of people prefer using **Sensing (S)***
*Approximately 25% prefer using **iNtuition (N)***

The following table illustrates the differences between **Sensing** and **iNtuition**.

TABLE: S AND N DATA GATHERING DIFFERENCES

SENSING (S):		INTUITION (N):
Through their five senses.	**How Do They Gather Information?**	Through a personal prism.
Things that can be seen, touched, tasted, smelled or heard.	**What Kind Of Information Do They Look For?**	Patterns and relationships between new information and what they know.
The details of what is going on around them.	**What are they Most Aware Of?**	How information is related to other things.
How something is relevant to them, what the rules are, and how things are supposed to be done.	**What Do They Want To Know?**	Why? Understand universal truths behind things to help them better understand the world.
On "What is!" They look for evidence and proof.	**Where do They Put Their Focus?**	On "What if?" They look for how things could be.
Facts and details that are personally relevant to them.	**What Do They Listen For?**	Interesting ideas and what is "possible."
Information about the past and the present.	**What Do They Focus On?**	Information about the future and the present.
By the accuracy of the facts and details.	**How Do They Judge Credibility?**	By the thought process, creativity and recognition of impacts on other things.
Simplicity.	**What Catches Their Attention?**	Complexity.

As you can see, **Sensors** and **iNtuitives** naturally notice different things and communicate information differently.

HOW SENSORS GATHER AND COMMUNICATE INFORMATION

Sensing means gathering information beginning with details, using the five senses -- what can be seen, touched, tasted, smelled, and heard.

Sensors need details to stay grounded. They like tangible proof of ideas and concepts.

Sensors are good at seeing things as they are and they tend to compare new things to their past experience. When asked to do something in a new way, they might resist – unless it is not working the current way. Their normal stance is, "If it ain't broke, don't fix it!" You will also sometimes hear a *Sensor* say, "We tried that before, it didn't work."

Sensors tend to be practical, down-to-earth and to offer a realistic appraisal of things. *Sensors* like details. They enjoy:

- ✓ Understanding exactly what is expected of them.

- ✓ Being told that they did a job correctly.

- ✓ Knowing that something is practical and useful to them before they pay much attention to it.

- ✓ Becoming expert in something by practicing it to build expertise.

HOW INTUITIVES GATHER AND COMMUNICATE INFORMATION

INtuitive means gathering information beginning with the big picture - using their "sixth sense" of how things fit together. *INtuitives* need context and want to understand why. They are good at seeing new possibilities and connections between issues. When asked to do something the same way, they may have difficulty or become bored. They are apt to say, "What if we tried doing it this way instead?" You will often hear an *iNtuitive* person use the words, "What if?"

INtuitives tend to be imaginative and to take a novel approach to things. They like the big picture. They enjoy:

- ✓ Understanding the "why" behind things.

- ✓ Understanding how things are interrelated, often connecting new information to things they already know about.

- ✓ Variety and novelty rather than repetition.

- ✓ Coming up with new ways of looking at things and doing familiar things a new way.

SENSORS AND INTUITIVES UNDER STRESS

When stressed, people cannot process information as effectively;
this further impedes their ability to learn and to communicate.

Stress changes a person's ability to process information.

Sensing people who are stressed tend to lose track of the facts and instead imagine a worst case scenario. So, a person who is talking about how everything is falling apart at the seams may be a **Sensor** who is stressed.

INtuitive people might focus on a detail when stressed and lose sight of the big picture. A person who is harping on a detail may well be an **iNtuitive** under stress.

STRESS IN SENSORS (S):

Sensors who are stressed may forget things or lose things, rather than being able to easily notice and remember the important details of their life. They may theorize about why things are not as they "should" be. Or they may worry about everything going wrong.

To deal more effectively with stress, **Sensors** need to get back to the facts. Rather than worrying about what *might* happen or what *might* go wrong, they need to focus on what *actually is* happening. Sensors process information better when they focus on the present moment rather than speculating about the future.

Because **iNtuitives** naturally look to the future, they might engage a stressed **Sensor** in conversation about all the alternatives, believing this will help! Instead, talk with them about things in the past that worked out even though they worried about them. Focus on the facts, rather than what might be happening.

When a person is predicting a negative outcome for the future
it is often a sign of a Sensor under stress.

STRESS IN INTUITIVES (N):

iNtuitives who are stressed may become obsessed with a detail that is not "right." It is as though they cannot see the forest because there is a large tree standing right in front of them, obscuring everything else. They may talk or think obsessively about one fact or lose their usual ability to see plenty of options.

To deal more effectively with stress, they need to either step away from the situation or talk with someone who can help put things into perspective. They need to focus on what is possible and what is working rather than focusing on the one detail that is not right.

Because **Sensors** naturally deal with details, they might try to engage the stressed person by offering suggestions for fixing the detail, thinking this will help! Instead, acknowledge the snag and remind them that the answer will come to them.

> *When a person is stuck on a fact and only seeing the negative in any given situation, it is often a sign of an iNtuitive under stress.*

USING KNOWLEDGE OF S AND N TO GET ALONG WITH OTHERS

iNtuitives pay attention to concepts and connections between things and might gloss over the details.

If you are an *iNtuitive* and you want to communicate with a **Sensor**, use:

- ✓ Examples to illustrate your points.
- ✓ Physical mock-ups of your ideas to allow them to use their senses to understand what you are talking about.
- ✓ Stories about others who have been successful implementing similar ideas.
- ✓ Details to make things more concrete and help Sensors evaluate your information.

Sensors pay attention to facts and details and notice what is going on around them. They might not be as interested in why things are that way or how they could be.

If you are a **Sensor** and want to communicate with an *iNtuitive Type*:

- ✓ Determine the purpose of your story, presentation or conversation and provide that up-front to the iNtuitive.
- ✓ Consider asking them about connections they see to other issues.
- ✓ Use questions to engage them and stimulate their natural curiosity.

> *Communication leads to community, that is, to understanding,*
> *intimacy and mutual valuing. Rollo May*

To communicate most effectively with the widest possible audience, blend these two preferences – just as they do in a newspaper article.

1. Begin with the big picture. A newspaper will summarize the entire story, and why you want to know about it, in the headline and the first paragraph. This provides the context that iNtuitives need to understand the details. It is not so long-winded so as to lose the attention of the Sensors.

2. Then communicate the details. Step by step and bit by bit. Make sure you have them right!

3. Then close by summarizing what was said and why it was important. This guides everyone to the conclusions that you've drawn from your concepts and supporting data.

Now you've discovered the differences in how people naturally gather information. You can use what you've learned to improve communication and to reduce the stress in all of your relationships.

S and N EXAMPLE

Husband Jim and wife Mary were at a social function and Jim was recounting a recent, interesting experience.

Jim, an *iNtuitive*, was focused on making the story interesting as he wove together fact and fantasy. Mary, a Sensor, kept interrupting him because he couldn't seem to keep the facts straight!   Exasperated with the interruptions Jim finally said, "Fine, YOU tell the story!" Jim was trying to use their experience to make a point about things in general; Mary was focused on the details of what actually happened. Her version of the story did not meet his objective and she did not have fun telling it.

It was a long ride home that night.

Next, in in-depth look at the third letter of Personality Type – The Mode of Operating you use to make decisions!

Chapter 7 – Your Decision Making Mode of Operating

Much of the stress in any relationship comes from believing that others see things the way we do, or that that they should. Understanding how people naturally differ when making decisions helps overcome misunderstandings.

The third letter of your Personality Type indicates your preferred Mode of operating when making decisions. This affects the way you process everything going on around you.

Thinking deciders tend to pay more attention to tasks and things.

Feeling deciders tend to pay more attention to people and relationships.

Again, we all make decisions using *both **Thinking and Feeling***, but we naturally rely on one more than the other to guide us.

<u>WHY UNDERSTANDING DECISION MAKING IS IMPORTANT</u>

If you ever wonder how in the world others come to their conclusions or if you can't seem to persuade others when you disagree, it may be a matter of hard-wired differences.

T – Thinkers and F – Feelers:

- ✓ Look at problems differently.
- ✓ Evaluate opportunities differently.
- ✓ Pay attention to different types of criteria.

DECISION MAKING ISSUES ARISE WHEN:

People use different criteria to evaluate problems and opportunities and cannot understand how the other person could arrive at "that" decision.

ARE YOU PRIMARILY THINKING (T) OR FEELING (F)?

This is the only factor of Personality Type that appears to have a gender bias.

MEN: *Approximately 75% naturally prefer making decisions using **Thinking;** 25% naturally prefer making decisions using **Feeling.***

WOMEN: *Approximately 75% naturally prefer making decisions using **Feeling;** 25% naturally prefer making decisions using **Thinking.***

The following table illustrates the differences between *Thinking* and *Feeling.*

TABLE: T AND F DECISION MAKING DIFFERENCES

THINKING (T):		FEELING (F):
Projects, tasks and analysis.	**Where is their Focus?**	People, relationships and values.
Objectively and dispassionately.	**How do they view the world?**	Subjectively and passionately.
Like "the right" decisions. They believe there is one way -- an almost mathematical way -- to decide things.	**How do they gauge whether a decision is good?**	Believe a decision should be "fair." They especially like to find "win-win" scenarios.
Are they competent?	**How do they Evaluate others?**	Are they compassionate?
People are taking things "too personally."	**How do they decide that things are going wrong?**	People are "cold and uncaring" when deciding things.
Once made, a decision should be easy to implement because it just "makes sense."	**How do they approach implementing decisions?**	Decisions would be easier to implement if the people actually cared about those involved.
Talk about tasks, projects and things.	**What type of language do they use?**	Talk about people, impacts, values and relationships.

As you can see, people naturally notice different aspects of decisions and tend to decide from that perspective. Even if Thinkers and Feelers make the same decision, they come to that decision from different perspectives.

HOW THINKERS DECIDE

Thinking means deciding things logically and objectively. *Thinking* deciders approach problems in a scientific or mathematical way. They like to analyze facts and data. They look at decisions dispassionately, easily identifying the pros and cons of any issue. When they reach a conclusion, they are likely to believe it is the "right" answer and are persuaded only by new information.

You can rely upon a *Thinking* decider to look at problems analytically. They like to:

- ✓ Understand what is wrong with any given scenario.
- ✓ Ask questions to clarify information.
- ✓ Argue using logic.
- ✓ Develop and use problem solving models.
- ✓ Compare and contrast options, evaluating alternatives analytically.

HOW FEELERS DECIDE

Feeling means making decisions from a relationship standpoint. *Feeling* deciders try to "walk in everyone's shoes" so they can understand how those involved are affected. They approach decisions empathetically and compassionately. They look for what is working and ways to build on that.

You can rely upon a *Feeling* decider to work diligently to find solutions that will promote harmony and get everyone "on the same page." They like to:

- ✓ Understand each person's values and priorities and how they feel about a situation.
- ✓ Avoid arguments and keep things positive.
- ✓ Consider the nuances of situations given the people who are involved.
- ✓ Minimize disagreements and focus on consensus.

We are the creative force of our life, and through our own decisions rather than our conditions, if we carefully learn to do certain things, we can accomplish those goals. Stephen Covey

---

HOW BOTH TS AND FS CAN MAKE BETTER DECISIONS

There is a way to ensure you make the best decisions, personal or professional! The best decisions take into account all four Modes of Operating:

- ✓ **Both** modes of gathering information: *Sensing (S)* and *iNtuition (N)*.

- ✓ **Both** modes of making decisions: *Thinking (T)* and *Feeling (F)*.

Because you naturally pay closer attention to your Best Mode and your secondary mode, you will need to concentrate on paying attention to your third and fourth modes of operating.

If you naturally pay closer attention to *Sensing,* you may miss the big picture. If you naturally pay closer attention to *iNtuition*, you might miss important details.

If you naturally pay more attention to *Thinking,* you might miss important interpersonal implications of a decision. If you naturally pay closer attention to *Feeling*, you might miss some of the logic or pros and cons of various options.

Considering aspects which run counter to your natural hard-wiring may be difficult at first. You can either consciously stretch to consider them or you can ask for advice or input from someone who has strengths that are opposite yours.

Use the following Problem Solving model and notice how much confidence you gain when making decisions - knowing you have looked things from all angles.

PROBLEM SOLVING MODEL

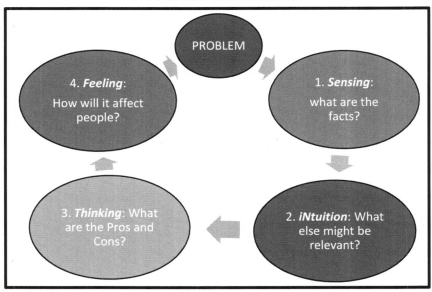

THINKERS AND FEELERS UNDER STRESS

---

*People who are stressed lose their ability to evaluate situations the
way they usually do, hampering their ability to decide.*

Stress changes a person's ability to make decisions.

> ➤ **Thinkers** who are stressed become hypersensitive to criticism and
> over-react to people's feelings, instead of deciding logically like they
> usually do. So, a person who is dismayed by interpersonal issues may
> be a **Thinker** under stress.

> ➤ **Feelers** who are stressed become picky, critical, and cynical instead of
> deciding based on what is best for people like they usually do. A person
> who is snarky and negative may be a **Feeler** under stress.

STRESS IN THINKERS (T):

When **Thinking** deciders are stressed, they may become overwhelmed by
feelings of self-doubt and become hypersensitive to the criticism of others. They
may see others as having ulterior motives or as being "needy" of too much
attention from them.

To deal more effectively with stress, **Thinkers** need to get back to the logic of the
situation rather than focusing on their negative feelings and relationship
problems. They need to focus on the pros and cons of the situation, develop
logical alternatives and objectively decide how to proceed.

Because **Feeling** deciders are naturally concerned with how others are being
impacted by things, they might try to engage a stressed **Thinker** in a discussion
of their feelings or relationships, believing this will help.

Instead, give them positive feedback and support and then focus on the pros and
cons of the situation.

---

*When a person is uncharacteristically emotional or doubting their
own viewpoint, it is often a sign of a Thinker under stress.*

STRESS IN FEELERS (F):

When *Feeling* deciders are stressed, they may become overwhelmed with negativity and focus on what is going wrong rather than being concerned with supporting others as they usually are. They may become more focused than usual on themselves, and view others as "dragging them down."

To deal more effectively with stress, *Feelers* need to focus on supporting and helping others rather than expecting things from them. They need to remember that it is their relationships that are most important to them and decide what they can do to get everyone back in harmony.

Because *Thinking* deciders are naturally critical and skeptical, they might want to help the *Feeler* solve the problem by analyzing what is wrong with the situation, thinking that will help!

Instead, reconnect with them in a personal way, showing them that you care about them and helping them put things back into perspective.

> *When a person is negatively hypercritical,*
> *it is often a sign of a Feeler under stress.*

USING KNOWLEDGE OF T AND F TO GET ALONG BETTER WITH OTHERS

Understanding the in-born differences in how people make decisions can help avoid many misunderstandings and improve your ability to understand and interact with others.

IF YOU ARE A THINKER, it is important to realize that Feelers believe that smooth-running relationships are key to everything. A Feeling decider is wired to want a "win-win" solution. Feelers may be so focused on relationships that they have difficulty moving forward unless they feel the people involved are happy and engaged.

They enjoy knowing that everyone is on the same page and that people are enjoying working together toward a common goal. If people are not expressing positive feelings, they may believe there is something wrong and want to fix the relationship or change things so that everyone is OK. They may also think that criticism of their ideas means you do not value them.

> *Thinkers can improve their relationships by being more open*
> *with positive thoughts and feelings. Think of the people*
> *around you as important "projects" that require your*
> *attention and effort.*

IF YOU ARE A FEELER, it is important to understand that Thinkers may be so focused on what they are working on (a project or even a thought) that they forget to thank people or express satisfaction with them. Thinking deciders may be so absorbed in figuring something out that they appear to be "upset." Often they are only wrestling with the problem and unaware of interpersonal implications of their actions.

They are hard-wired to see what is wrong so they can fix it. If they are not pointing out something that is wrong, then things are probably fine. They do not tend to use a lot of adjectives or talk about people in glowing terms.

> *Feelers can improve all their relationships by being more aware and accepting of people who are not as comfortable expressing their feelings. Get to know each individual's signs of feeling satisfied rather than expecting Feeling-type feedback from them.*

T and F EXAMPLE

Mark and Jim were working on a project together for the first time. Mark (a *T*) thought they should begin by doing some research – looking at the data and documenting the pros and cons of various alternatives. Jim (an *F*) also wanted to begin with some research. He wanted to interview the people involved to determine their issues. Instead of arguing about which approach to take, they agreed that each should proceed researching independently and they would meet a week later to review their results.

Together they learned far more about the problems, the alternatives and workable solutions than either of them would have on their own. And, they gained respect for what each of them brought to the project.

Now that you understand the first three letters of your Personality type, it is time to move to the last letter – HOW YOU PRIORITIZE YOUR LIFE.

Chapter 8 – How You Prioritize Your Life

Many people are stressed because they cannot get everything done!
Understanding how your mind views priorities can help you
effectively deal with this common stress.

The last letter of your Personality Type indicates how you prioritize. This affects the way you approach getting things done, and is readily visible to others. Understanding this concept will change the way you approach many aspects of your life.

WHY UNDERSTANDING HOW YOU PRIORITIZE IS IMPORTANT

Why is this important? Because we all have so many things we want to accomplish, and we have limited time and energy to get it all done.

When this letter is not understood, it often causes either self-doubt or frustration with others. Many conflicts between people are the result of differences in how they prioritize or what they view as most important.

If you have ever wondered why some people are organized and others seem to lack structure, it is probably a matter of hard-wiring. People are naturally wired to prioritize in one of two ways, either *Judging (J) or Perceiving (P).*

Judgers (J) naturally prefer structure in their lives. They like:

- ✓ Routines and schedules.

- ✓ Being able to work on one thing at a time, checking each one off their list.

- ✓ To be organized.

- ✓ To make decisions and move on.

Perceivers (P) naturally prefer flexibility. They like:

- ✓ To have freedom to work on what inspires them, juggling many projects, moving from one to another easily.

- ✓ Flexibility and spontaneity.

- ✓ To occasionally organize things when inspired to do so.

- ✓ To gather information and explore the options.

ARE YOU JUDGING (J) OR PERCEIVING (P)?

*Approximately 50% of people naturally prefer **Judging (J)***
*Approximately 50% of people naturally prefer **Perceiving (P)***

Understanding the in-born differences in how people prioritize their lives can help avoid feelings of guilt as well as conflict between individuals. Do you wonder why some people are always on the go without any free time in their schedules, while others seem to "go with the flow?" Have you noticed that some people are up all night finishing an important project, while others finish things early? It is likely a matter of hard-wiring.

Understanding the differences in how people are hard-wired to prioritize is key to self-management and to living and working with others.

The following table illustrates the differences between **Judging** and **Perceiving**.

TABLE: J AND P PRIORITIZING DIFFERENCES

JUDGERS (J):		PERCEIVERS (P):
Make decisions and move on!	**What are they driven to do?**	Explore options and gather information.
Finishing things! Practicing and perfecting something more than continually being asked to do something different.	**What do they enjoy?**	Starting things! New projects more than practicing and perfecting something they have done before.
By planning and scheduling what they will do and when.	**How do they get the most done?**	By working on the project that is most inspiring or has the closest deadline.
They like routine; they don't like interruptions or surprises. Checking things off their list is motivating; unfinished tasks "hang over their heads."	**What motivates them?**	They like variety, new experiences and surprises. Inspiration, deadlines and new tasks draw their attention.

As you can see, people are naturally motivated differently. Understanding this will alleviate stress. You will be able to manage yourself in accordance with your own hard-wiring and you will better understand others.

HOW JUDGERS PRIORITIZE

Judging means prioritizing things in a structured, organized and efficient way.

Judgers like to plan, organize, schedule and then execute tasks – preferably one at a time! They like to finish things, getting them done and checked off their list. And yes, they do HAVE a list! They like the feeling of being in control of their lives! They like predictability, knowing what to expect and getting things done. And they also DO get lots of things done!

You can rely upon a Judger to be efficient. They like:

- ✓ Rules and procedures, and will likely follow them.

- ✓ Making "to do" lists.

- ✓ Master calendars and day planners for keeping track of their important projects and commitments.

- ✓ Thinking about how they will approach something before they begin - usually outlining all the steps in their optimal order.

- ✓ Getting things done NOW! Unfinished work bothers them until it is finished.

If you are a *Judger*, you may be surprised to learn that only half of the population is wired that way! If you are living or working with a *Perceiver*, their inability to plan ahead, organize or live by a schedule might be a source of frustration and conflict. By now you realize you cannot change them into a *Judger*, right? What can you do?

Help them keep their deadlines visible and help them get excited about things that are important. Remember, *Perceivers* are motivated by inspiration and deadlines rather than schedules and checking things off a list like you are.

HOW PERCEIVERS PRIORITIZE

Perceiving means prioritizing according to the closest deadline or what is most inspiring at the moment.

Perceivers like to explore options, examine alternatives and work inspirationally. They usually have many unfinished projects and find they get much more done when they are facing a deadline or really motivated to work on it. They like to work under pressure because their mind focuses better. They like the freedom and flexibility to put effort into the thing that most appeals to them at the time. They often find new ways of doing things because they are hard-wired for exploring options rather than finishing things.

You can rely on a **Perceiver** to explore options and to focus in a crisis. They like:

- ✓ The freedom to decide what to do and when.
- ✓ Trying new ways of doing things.
- ✓ Jumping into a project and seeing where it goes.
- ✓ Adapting to changing circumstances.
- ✓ Experimenting and learning.
- ✓ Surprises!

If you are a **Perceiver**, you may be surprised to find that half the population *is* wired like you! And you may be frustrated by **Judgers** in your life who are always over-scheduled, working all the time, and are stressed over everything that is still left to do. By now you realize you cannot change them into a **Perceiver**, right? What can you do?

Because **Judgers** love knowing what they are going to do ahead of time, you might try scheduling some time on their calendar for connecting with them. Make it clear that you are not exactly sure what type of activity you will share, but you are really looking forward to spending time with them!

HOW JUDGERS CAN GET BALANCE IN THEIR LIFE

Are you stressed because you feel you have too much to do? Most **Judgers** tell us they are! Here are some tips that work for **Judgers**!

Judgers often run themselves ragged because they like to get things "done" and "off their plate." They often plan and schedule virtually every possible minute of their day.

The first thing to realize is that not everything is equally important! Begin to prioritize things according to the Pareto Principle.

The Pareto Principle[2] concludes that 20% of your activities produce 80% of your results. Think about the Pareto Principle in terms of your experience, to prove to yourself that it is true.

---

[2] From Wikipedia: Business-management consultant Joseph M. Juran coined the term Pareto Principle (also known as the 80–20 rule) and named it after Italian economist Vilfredo Pareto. Pareto developed the principle by observing that 20% of the pea pods in his garden contained 80% of the peas. Many natural phenomena have been shown empirically to exhibit such a distribution.

You probably wear 20% of your clothes 80% of the time, you make 20% of your recipes 80% of the time, 20% of the people in your life provide you with 80% of your moral support. Got it?

Put your first effort into prioritizing things on your "to do" list.

You may be surprised to find that the things near the bottom of the list are either overtaken by events or will have lost their importance all together.

Which are the 20% that will produce 80% of your goals? Those things need to be at the top of your list.

And remember that taking time for yourself always needs to be in the top 20%!

The key is not to prioritize what's on your schedule, but to schedule your priorities. Stephen Covey

---

There are three important things to remember if you are a **Judger**.

1. No matter how much you get done in a day, there will probably *never* be a day when you can sit back and declare that you have done *everything*.

2. According to The Pareto Principle, 20% of the things on your "to do" list produce 80% of your results. So, the real key is stopping to prioritize. Learn to focus on the most important 20% and feel calm and satisfied knowing you have used your time most efficiently.

3. Then be sure to schedule time for yourself every day. When you feel rejuvenated, you are actually able to get more done. Taking care of yourself must *always* be on your list!

> *PRIORITY ISSUES ARISE WHEN:*
> *People have differing views on the use of resources (such as time or money) or how and when to get things done.*

HOW PERCEIVERS CAN GET THE IMPORTANT THINGS DONE

Often **Perceivers** beat themselves up for not being more structured and organized. They *try* to use day planners but find it is difficult for them.

If you are a **Perceiver** and live or work with a **Judger**, their constant level of activity might make you think you are "lazy" and their ability to get things done early, might make you think you are a "procrastinator."

What can you do?   First, realize that you have different strengths than the **Judgers** you know.

Your mind is always exploring and open to new opportunities. You probably work better under pressure or even when there is a crisis. Many emergency room doctors, nurses and technicians are **Perceivers**. Their minds are able to focus like a laser when there is pressure; **Judgers** minds scatter and lose focus under too much pressure.

*Follow your bliss and the universe will open doors
where there were only walls. Joseph Campbell*

There are three important things to consider if you are a **Perceiver**:

1. Create deadlines for your important tasks. As a deadline approaches, your mind will focus better. You may want to write the deadline on your calendar or make a commitment to someone else. When you make a commitment and set a deadline, your mind will focus like a laser beam and you will get it done on time.

2. Find the inspiration to complete a project. If you've lost motivation for a task, look for a way to get it back. If you are making a gift for someone, keep their picture handy to inspire you or think about how pleased they will be. Invite someone over so you are inspired to clean the house. Read something new or talk with someone new about a stale project to rekindle your interest.

3. Keep a simple and flexible stack of reminders of things you want or need to accomplish, rather than a list. Maybe a stack of 3x5 cards or notes on a tack board could help. When there is nothing specific drawing your attention and focus, look through the notes and choose something to do. Having the freedom to choose from a number of things will allow your mind to explore, become energized and then focus.

JUDGERS AND PERCEIVERS UNDER STRESS

Stress changes a person's ability to prioritize things the way they normally do.

> ➤ **Judgers** are usually quick to organize their activities and get things done but when stressed they may become confused and indecisive.

> ➤ **Perceivers** under stress may make snap decisions. By knowing when others are stressed, you can help them regain their ability to prioritize in ways that work for them.

People who are stressed have difficulty prioritizing their activities and achieving balance in their lives.

Stress In Judgers (J):

When under stress, **Judgers** often talk about being "overwhelmed" or "on overload." If they have too many things on their "to do" list they can become focused on what they are **not** getting done instead of everything they **are** getting done.

To deal more effectively with stress, **Judgers** need to build time into their schedule for themselves! When they are less stressed, they will actually get more done. Be sure the **Judgers** in your life are taking time away from their work to do something they enjoy. Recharging their energy will stave off stress.

Because **Perceivers** naturally juggle many things and do not feel as much stress from "unfinished" projects, they may downplay the anxiety by telling the **Judger** to lighten up! "It's no big deal!"

Instead, acknowledge how much they have accomplished and encourage them to take time for themselves to regroup. They will be able to attack the list with renewed fervor when they are fresh!

When a person feels overwhelmed by all they have to do,
it is often a sign of a Judger in stress.

STRESS IN PERCEIVERS (P):

When under stress, **Perceivers** might uncharacteristically panic and worry about all the things they have started that are not finished. They may complain about how lazy and disorganized they are.

To deal more effectively with stress, **Perceivers** need to get the important things done on time. You can help the **Perceivers** in your life prioritize things and keep their deadlines and important projects visible.

Because **Judgers** are naturally good at rolling up their sleeves and getting things done, they may try to help the **Perceiver** finish the project at hand. The problem is, the project at hand might not be the highest priority! First, help them prioritize. Then your efforts can actually help them reduce stress.

When a person makes snap judgments and tries to finish the first thing that pops into their head, it is often a sign of a Perceiver in stress.

J and P EXAMPLE

Pat (**Perceiver)** and her husband Jack (**Judger)** had plans to leave by car on a long trip. Jack wanted to leave no later than 7am so they would arrive at their first overnight stop before he was too tired. He jumped out of bed at 5, took his shower, packed his shaving kit and loaded the car with everything he and Pat had staged by the door the day before. He was ready to go with plenty of time to enjoy a cup of coffee while Pat assembled her last minute items. Surprised at not hearing her scurrying around, he went to check. She was still sleeping! "Pat, get up! I'm ready to leave!" "What time is it?" she asked him. "It's 6:30! We are leaving at 7!" Pat sprang into action, noticing several things she wished she had packed the day before. She grabbed another duffle bag and filled it. "Better water the plants. Better take the bills along. Where's that bag I like for carrying paperwork? Oh well, they will fit in this shopping bag just fine." "OK", she exclaims as she arrives in the kitchen loaded down with bags at 7:15, and pleased with herself for being so punctual. "I'm ready!"

Jack was not amused. Where is he going to put all *that* stuff? To him, she is a scatter-brained, unorganized procrastinator who needs to "grow up!" Pat cannot understand why he is so uptight! "It's not the end of the world!" she thinks. "All he does is pick at me. It seems I can never do anything right!"

You now have a better understanding of the people who are wired differently from you. Next, we will look at how these four letters combine to produce the 16 unique Personality Types.

Chapter 9 – Understanding the 16 Personality Types

If one does not understand a person,
one tends to regard him as a fool. Carl Jung

In previous Chapters, we discussed the natural, inborn preferences which form the basis of any given individual's Personality Type. We also discovered that while people physically react to stress in the same way, they react mentally based upon their Personality Type. By understanding all 16 Personality Types, you will not only be able to reduce your own stress, you will also begin to recognize when others are stressed. And you will be able to use this information to improve your relationships with all types of people.

Before moving on, let's do a quick review of the letters that comprise Personality type.

➤ The first letter is either **E or I.** The first letter indicates whether you prefer **Extraversion (E)** or **Introversion (I). Extraverts** recharge their energy by active interaction with people and **Introverts** recharge by spending time by themselves doing something they enjoy.

➤ The second letter is either **S or N.** The second letter addresses the two Modes people prefer to gather information. **Sensors (S)** begin with the details while **iNtuitives (N)** begin with the big picture.

➤ The third letter is either **T or F.** The third letter depicts the two Modes people prefer to make decisions. **Thinkers (T)** like to decide objectively and analytically while **Feelers (F)** like to decide compassionately.

➤ The fourth Letter is either **J or P.** The last letter illustrates how you prioritize your life -- whether you outwardly prefer decision making or data gathering. **Judgers (J)** prioritize using efficiency and prefer to make decisions, getting things done and off their list. **Perceivers (P)** prioritize inspirationally, preferring to begin new projects, gather more information and explore options.

PUTTING THE LETTERS TOGETHER

As you know, the four letters of an individual's in-born preferences, become their Personality Type. There are 16 Personality Types and each one has strengths and stressors that are predictable. We've given each of the 16 Personality Types a nickname to depict their dominant characteristics. All 16 Personality Types and their nicknames are displayed on the following table.

Locate your Personality Type on the table below.

By looking closely at the nicknames, you will begin to see the differences in Personality Types. A "Healer," for example, is only one letter different from an "Architect" yet you can begin to imagine how different those two Types are!

TABLE: ALL 16 PERSONALITY TYPES

		Sensing		iNtuitive	
		Thinking	Feeling	Feeling	Thinking
Introverts	Judging	**ISTJ** "The Duty-Bound Inspector"	**ISFJ** "The Always Ready Helper"	**INFJ** "The Persistent Counselor"	**INTJ** "The Mastermind of Perfection"
Introverts	Perceiving	**ISTP** "The Independent Technician"	**ISFP** "The Caring Facilitator"	**INFP** "The Unassuming Healer"	**INTP** "The Architect in Search of Inspiration"
Extroverts	Perceiving	**ESTP** "The Irresistible Promoter"	**ESFP** "The On Stage Improviser"	**ENFP** "The Champion of Important Causes"	**ENTP** "The Inventor of Interesting Solutions"
Extroverts	Judging	**ESTJ** "The Supervisor of Practical Projects"	**ESFJ** "The Quintessential Provider"	**ENFJ** "The Ever Devoted, Sensitive Teacher"	**ENTJ** "The Spontaneous Leader for Every Occasion"

Each Introvert and Sensing Type (ISTJ, ISFJ, ISTP and ISFP) is approximately 5% of the population.

Each Introvert and iNtuitive Type (INFJ, INTJ, INFP and INTP) is approximately 1% of the population.

Each Extravert and Sensing Type (ESTP, ESFP, ESTJ and ESFJ) is approximately 15% of the population.

Each Extravert and iNtuitive Type (ENFP, ENTP, ENFJ and ENTJ) is approximately 5% of the population.

Chapter 10 - ISTJs and ISFJs under Stress

Under stress ISFJs and ISTJs, tend to catastrophize about the future. Why?

Normally both of these Personality Types are grounded in the details – their Best Mode of Operating is *Sensing*. They are *Introverts* so they naturally focus on remembering and cataloguing those details inside their heads.

ISTJs can remember and recite the time, date and perhaps even the weather conditions, for any important day in their past. As "T"s, they are focused on the facts surrounding all of the projects and tasks that are important to them. It is as though their brain contains a giant filing cabinet where the detailed files are stored neatly away and can be pulled out instantly and recounted with tremendous accuracy.

Similarly, ISFJs remember all the relevant facts about the people they care about. As "F"s they focus on relationships. Every birthday, every gift, every important conversation, even facial expressions – all are stored in their highly detail-oriented brain.

When stressed, the body reacts by going into "Fight or Flight." And, the brain shuts down – switching to its most primitive way of operating. There is no time to process things, the brain reasons, there is an emergency, just REACT! The least effective mode of operating for ISTJ and ISFJ is their iNtuition. And, because they are Introverts, their stress is Extraverted; they talk about it and it shows!

When stressed ISTJs and ISFJs lose track of their Sensing details and become overwhelmed by the iNtuitive possibilities of what might go wrong! They see a big picture of doom and gloom.

They lose their connection with the past and all they know, and automatically react by worrying about the future.

Sound familiar?

If you are ISTJ or ISFJ (or you know someone who is) what can you do?

Follow these steps to return to balance.

1. Learn to recognize your Stress Mode: ***EXTRAVERTED INTUITION***.

   Whenever you notice that you are:
   - ✓ Having an outburst of negativity or panic,
   - ✓ Talking about how things might go wrong,
   - ✓ Worrying about the future.

STOP and notice that these are just signs that you are stressed; this is not who you are! There is nothing wrong with you; it is simply your mind's way of letting you know that you are stressed.

2. Understand the "true" source of your stress.

    Often people believe stress is caused by an external situation or person. In truth, people *react* differently to the same situations, so it can't be caused by the situation. Therefore, recognize it is your automatic, inborn, hard-wired *reaction* to the situation or person that actually causes you to experience the "Fight or Flight" response and its negative physical, mental and emotional effects.

    The underlying "hard-wiring" of your mind, as an ISTJ or ISFJ, predicts that you will automatically react by "freaking out," worrying about the future.

    When you recognize your signs of stress, you can choose to **STOP** the automatic, hard-wired responses, and take back control of your emotions and behavior. Understanding the true source of your stress gives you the power to choose how to act in the face of stress.

3. As soon as you recognize you are in your "Stress Mode," STOP and take a few slow, deep breaths.

    Breathe in through your nose as if you are breathing air into your stomach and then out through your mouth.

    This is called deep breathing, conscious breathing or diaphragmatic breathing. This causes an automatic "Relaxation Response" in your body and your mind, which counteracts the "Fight or Flight" response.

4. Once you have relaxed your mind and body, consciously "shift" to your "Best Mode" - *INTROVERTED SENSING*.

    ✓   Stop talking and, if possible, get by yourself. Bring your focus back to the present moment.

    ✓   Ask yourself, "What are the facts?" Not what you think *might* happen! What do you actually *know* to be true? Remind yourself that dreaming up the worst case scenario is just a sign of stress. And look back at the facts and remember that most of the things you've worried about in the past never actually happened.

You got it! You are now in control!

Go to www.Lulu.com and type in "Stress Reduction Guide" to get the Guide for your Type. It includes your driving force, 4 inborn strengths and 4 strategies to reduce your stress and enhance your relationships.

Chapter 11 - INFJs and INTJs under Stress

Under stress INTJs and INFJs, tend to become overwhelmed by details. Why?

Normally both of these Personality Types are guided by their ability to see the big picture and how everything fits together. Their Best Mode of Operating is **iNtuition**. They are **Introverts** who naturally focus on figuring out solutions for complex issues. When they are stressed, it is usually because one little detail just does not fit!

INTJs are focused on solving problems. As "T"s, they are usually focused on technical problems that others find insurmountable. They do not necessarily see the answer immediately, but their brains work tirelessly to connect the dots and see solutions others cannot readily see.

Similarly, INFJs are focused on understanding and documenting the principles that guide people. As "F"s they are focused on making the world a better place – no simple task!

When stressed, the body reacts by going into "Fight or Flight." And, the brain shuts down – switching to its most primitive way of operating. There is no time to process things, the brain reasons, there is an emergency, just REACT! The least effective mode of operating for INTJ and INFJ is their Sensing – the opposite of their highly developed iNtuition. And, because they are Introverts, their stress is Extraverted; they talk about it and it shows!

When stressed INTJs and INFJs lose track of the big picture and become overwhelmed by one or more details that just don't fit! They see these details as huge obstacles to finding a solution. They lose their perspective and automatically react by obsessing over the details.

Sound familiar?

Follow these steps to return to balance.

If you are INTJ or INFJ (or you know someone who is) what can you do? Follow these steps to return to balance.

1. Learn to recognize your Stress Mode -- **EXTRAVERTED SENSING**.

    Whenever you notice that you are:
    ✓   Giving up or talking about how something is NOT working.

    ✓   Hyper-focused on a single detail.

    ✓   Unable to see the big picture and put things into perspective.

    ✓   Noticing only the flaws in a situation or person.

STOP and notice that these are just signs that you are stressed; this is not who you are! There is nothing wrong with you; it is simply your mind's way of letting you know that I am stressed.

2. Understand the "true" source of your stress.

    Often people believe stress is caused by an external situation or person. In truth, people *react* differently to the same situations, so stress cannot be caused by the situation. Therefore, recognize it is your automatic, inborn, hard-wired *reaction* to the situation or person that actually causes you to experience the "Fight or Flight" response and its negative physical, mental and emotional effects.

    The underlying "hard-wiring" of your mind, as an INTJ or INFJ, predicts that you will automatically react by "becoming bore-sighted," being overwhelmed by a detail.

    Once you become aware of your particular stress triggers, you can more easily and quickly identify when you are in your "Stress Mode."

    When you recognize your signs of stress, you can choose to **STOP** the automatic, hard-wired responses, and take back control of your emotions and behavior.

    Understanding the true source of your stress gives you the power to choose how to act in the face of stress.

3. As soon as you recognize you are in your "Stress Mode," STOP and take a few slow, deep breaths.

    Breathe in through your nose as if you are breathing air into your stomach and then out through your mouth.

    This is called deep breathing, conscious breathing or diaphragmatic breathing. This causes an automatic "Relaxation Response" in your body and your mind, which counteracts the "Fight or Flight" response.

4. Once you have relaxed your mind and body, consciously "shift" to your "Best Mode" - **INTROVERTED INTUITION.**

✓   Stop talking when you notice you are being negative rather than constructive.

✓   Walk away when you become frustrated with a project and go do something else. Realize that solutions do always come to you!

You got it! You are now in control!

Go to www.Lulu.com and type in "Stress Reduction Guide" to get the Guide for your Type. It includes your driving force, 4 inborn strengths and 4 strategies to reduce your stress and enhance your relationships.

Chapter 12 - ISFPs and INFPs under Stress

When stressed ISFPs and INFPs tend to be awash in negative thoughts. Why?

Normally both of these Personality Types are guided by their strong people-oriented values and a desire to help others. Their Best Mode of Operating is *Feeling*. They are *Introverts* who naturally focus on people.

ISFPs are focused on doing practical things for people. As "SF"s, they are usually focused on keeping everyone working together and solving the little issues that keep the job from getting done or keep people from getting along.

INFPs are focused on ideals. They are often the biggest supporter of any underdog and they notice who feels especially lost or requires support and help. As "NF"s they are focused on making the world a better place for people.

For INFPs and ISFPs, conflict is a huge stressor. They lose their ability to help others and their sense of purpose. They become so engrossed in the negativity that they begin to see everything as another example of what is wrong.

When stressed, the body reacts by going into "Fight or Flight." And, the brain shuts down – switching to its most primitive way of operating. There is no time to process things, the brain reasons, there is an emergency, just REACT! The least effective mode of operating for ISFP and INFP is their Thinking – the opposite of their highly developed Feeling. And, because they are Introverts, their stress is Extraverted; they talk about it and it shows!

When stressed ISFPs and INFPs lose track of the values that ground them and become focused on what is wrong with everything and everyone around them! They see only problems, becoming uncharacteristically picky and negative.

Sound familiar?

If you are ISFP or INFP (or you know someone who is) what can you do?

Follow these steps to return to balance.

1. Learn to recognize your Stress Mode -- **EXTRAVERTED THINKING**.

    Whenever you notice that you are:

    ✓   Lashing out critically at the ones you love.

    ✓   Being cynical.

    ✓   Focusing on your problems rather than what you can do to help others.

    ✓   Being negative instead of positive about your life and relationships.

From Stressed To Best   Page 68

STOP and notice that these are just signs that you are stressed; this is not who you are! There is nothing wrong with you; it is simply your mind's way of letting you know that you are stressed.

2. Understand the "true" source of your stress.

Often people believe stress is caused by an external situation or person. In truth, people *react* differently to the same situations, so stress cannot be caused by the situation. Therefore, recognize it is your automatic, inborn, hard-wired *reaction* to the situation or person that actually causes you to experience the "Fight or Flight" response and its negative physical, mental and emotional effects.

The underlying "hard-wiring" of your mind, as an ISFP or INFP, predicts that you will automatically react by becoming critical, negative, cynical and picky.

When you recognize your signs of stress, you can choose to **STOP** the automatic, hard-wired responses, and take back control of your emotions and behavior. Understanding the true source of your stress gives you the power to choose how to act in the face of stress.

3. As soon as you recognize you are in your "Stress Mode," STOP and take a few slow, deep breaths.

Breathe in through your nose as if you are breathing air into your stomach and then out through your mouth.

This is called deep breathing, conscious breathing or diaphragmatic breathing. This causes an automatic "Relaxation Response" in your body and your mind, which counteracts the "Fight or Flight" response.

4. Once you have relaxed your mind and body, consciously "shift" to your "Best Mode" - **INTROVERTED FEELING.**

✓ Stop talking and get by yourself if possible.

✓ Rather than thinking about everything that is wrong, focus on the things that you are grateful for!

✓ Go do something that reconnects your with people you care about and reminds you how much you love to support something bigger than yourself!

You got it! You are now in control!

Go to www.Lulu.com and type in "Stress Reduction Guide" to get the Guide for your Type. It includes your driving force, 4 inborn strengths and 4 strategies to reduce your stress and enhance your relationships.

Chapter 13 - ISTPs and INTPs under Stress

Under stress ISTPs and INTPs, tend to be overcome with emotion. Why?

Normally both of these Personality Types are grounded by an ability to go with the flow and look at things rationally. Their Best Mode of Operating is *Thinking*. They are *Introverts* who naturally focus on quietly figuring things out.

ISTPs are focused on doing practical things independently. They are not normally emotionally needy. As "S"s, they are usually focused on fixing things or making things, usually enjoying working on something tangible.

Similarly, INTPs are focused on independently developing ideas. As "N"s they are focused on solving problems that require their unique ability to see things differently.

For ISTPs and INTPs, emotions are unsettling. They lose their usual ability to let things go and they feel overcome by emotion. They become so emotional that they lose their ability to analyze and look objectively at the situation. Why?

When stressed, the body reacts by going into "Fight or Flight." And, the brain shuts down – switching to its most primitive way of operating. There is no time to process things, the brain reasons, there is an emergency, just REACT! The least effective mode of operating for ISTP and INTP is their **Feeling** – the opposite of their highly developed **Thinking**. And, because they are Introverts, their stress is Extraverted; they talk about it and it shows!

When stressed ISTPs and INTPs lose track of the logic of the situation that usually grounds them and become overwhelmed by emotion. They feel sad, lonely, angry or hurt.

Sound familiar?

If you are ISTP or INTP (or you know someone who is) what can you do?

Follow these steps to return to balance.

1. Learn to recognize your Stress Mode -- **EXTRAVERTED FEELING**.

    Whenever you notice that you are:

    ✓ Becoming overwhelmed with emotions.

    ✓ Obsessing over problems in a relationship.

    ✓ Lashing out emotionally.

STOP and notice that these are just signs that you are stressed; this is not who are! There is nothing wrong with you; it is simply your mind's way of letting you know that you are stressed.

2. Understand the "true" source of your stress.

   Often people believe stress is caused by an external situation or person. In truth, people react differently to the same situations, so stress cannot be caused by the situation. Therefore, recognize it is your automatic, inborn, hard-wired reaction to the situation or person that actually causes you to experience the "Fight or Flight" response and its negative physical, mental and emotional effects.

   The underlying "hard-wiring" of your mind, as an ISTP or INTP, predicts that you will automatically react by becoming visibly emotional.

   When you recognize your signs of stress, you can choose to **STOP** the automatic, hard-wired responses, and take back control of your emotions and behavior. Understanding the true source of your stress gives you the power to choose how to act in the face of stress.

3. As soon as you recognize you are in your "Stress Mode," STOP and take a few slow, deep breaths.

   ✓ Breathe in through your nose as if you are breathing air into your stomach and then out through your mouth.

   ✓ This is called deep breathing, conscious breathing or diaphragmatic breathing. This causes an automatic "Relaxation Response" in your body and your mind, which counteracts the "Fight or Flight" response.

4. Once you have relaxed your mind and body, consciously "shift" to your "Best Mode" - **INTROVERTED THINKING.**

   ✓ Get by yourself, if possible, and think about the situation logically!

   ✓ Remember all that you have accomplished.

   ✓ Recognize your own contributions.

   ✓ Remember that you are uniquely suited to do what you do.

You got it! You are now in control!

Go to www.Lulu.com and type in "Stress Reduction Guide" to get the Guide for your Type. It includes your driving force, 4 inborn strengths and 4 strategies to reduce your stress and enhance your relationships.

Chapter 14 - ESTPs and ESFPs under Stress

Under stress ESTPs and ESFPs, tend to withdraw and worry about the future. Why?

Normally both of these Personality Types are guided by their enthusiasm for exploring the world around them! Their Best Mode of Operating is *Sensing*. They are *Extraverts* who naturally love to experience everything life has to offer.

ESTPs are focused on getting others caught up in the excitement. As "ST"s, they are usually doing some exciting activity with others.

Similarly, ESFPs love the spotlight! They are supremely improvisational and always add a bit of fun and drama to any social gathering. As "SF"s they love to cheer people up and help them have fun!

For ESTPs and ESFPs, responsibility can become overwhelming. They lose their usual zest for life and fall prey to a sense of impending doom about the future.

When stressed, the body reacts by going into "Fight or Flight." And, the brain shuts down – switching to its most primitive way of operating. There is no time to process things, the brain reasons, there is an emergency, just REACT! The least effective mode of operating for ESTP and ESFP is their **iNtuition** – the opposite of their highly developed **Sensing**. And, because they are Extraverts, their stress is Introverted; they withdraw from the world and focus inside their heads!

When stressed ESTPs and ESFPs lose their energy, enthusiasm and desire to get out and do things with others. They become uncharacteristically sullen and quiet. They become worried about the future although they may not be able to put their figure on exactly why they feel that way.

Sound familiar?

If you are ESTP or ESFP (or you know someone who is) what can you do?

Follow these steps to return to balance.

1. Learn to recognize your Stress Mode -- **INTROVERTED INTUITION**.

    Whenever you notice that you are:

    ✓   Withdrawing from the world and not feeling like participating.

    ✓   Worrying about the future.

    ✓   Doubting your abilities.

    ✓   Having feelings of impending doom.

STOP and notice that these are just signs that you are stressed; this is not who you are! There is nothing wrong with you; it is simply your mind's way of letting you know that you are stressed.

2. Understand the "true" source of your stress.

   Often people believe stress is caused by an external situation or person. In truth, people react differently to the same situations, so stress cannot be caused by the situation. Therefore, recognize it is your automatic, inborn, hard-wired reaction to the situation or person that actually causes you to experience the "Fight or Flight" response and its negative physical, mental and emotional effects.

   The underlying "hard-wiring" of your mind, as an ESTP or ESFP, predicts that you will automatically react by withdrawing to worry about the future.

   When you recognize your signs of stress, you can choose to **STOP** the automatic, hard-wired responses, and take back control of your emotions and behavior. Understanding the true source of your stress gives you the power to choose how to act in the face of stress.

3. As soon as you recognize you are in your "Stress Mode," STOP and take a few slow, deep breaths.

   Breathe in through your nose as if you are breathing air into your stomach and then out through your mouth.

   This is called deep breathing, conscious breathing or diaphragmatic breathing. This causes an automatic "Relaxation Response" in your body and your mind, which counteracts the "Fight or Flight" response.

4. Once you have relaxed your mind and body, consciously "shift" to your "Best Mode" – **EXTRAVERTED SENSING.**

   ✓ Get outside and go do something!

   ✓ Bring your focus back to the present moment.

   ✓ Ask yourself, "What are the facts?" Instead of worrying about what might happen.

   ✓ Remind yourself that most of the things you worried about in the past never actually happened.

You got it! You are now in control!

Go to www.Lulu.com and type in "Stress Reduction Guide" to get the Guide for your Type. It includes your driving force, 4 inborn strengths and 4 strategies to reduce your stress and enhance your relationships.

Chapter 15 - ENFPs and ENTPs under Stress

Under stress ENFPs and ENTPs, tend to withdraw and rehash the past. Why? Normally both of these Personality Types are guided by their enthusiasm for the future. Their Best Mode of Operating is *iNtuition*. They are **Extraverts** who naturally focus on seeing what is possible.

ENFPs are focused on what is possible for people. As "F"s, they are usually creating visions of how the world could be and inspiring others to get on-board. Similarly, INTPs are focused on creating solutions for opportunities they notice in the world around them. As "NT"s they like to play with ideas are focused on seeing things from every angle and solving problems.

For ENFPs and ENTPs, failure is overwhelming. They lose their usual ability to see options and instead become paralyzed by examinations of the past. Why?

When stressed, the body reacts by going into "Fight or Flight." And, the brain shuts down – switching to its most primitive way of operating. There is no time to process things, the brain reasons, there is an emergency, just REACT! The least effective mode of operating for ENFP and ENTP is their **Sensing** – the opposite of their highly developed **iNtuition**. And, because they are Extraverts, their stress is Introverted; they withdraw from the world and focus inside their heads! When stressed ENFPs and ENTPs lose their energy, enthusiasm and forward-looking perspective. They become uncharacteristically sullen and quiet. They become obsessed with the past and with real or imagined physical pain or even the stuffiness of a room.

Sound familiar?

If you are ENFP or ENTP (or you know someone who is) what can you do?

Follow these steps to return to balance.

1. Learn to recognize your Stress Mode -- **INTROVERTED SENSING**.

    Whenever you notice that you are:

    ✓   Withdrawing from the world and not feeling like participating.

    ✓   Hyper-focusing on your body and its aches and pains.

    ✓   Hyper-focusing on the environment, such as the temperature, odors or sounds.

    ✓   Rewinding and rehashing the details of the past.

STOP and notice that these are just signs that you are stressed; this is not who you are! There is nothing wrong with you; it is simply your mind's way of letting you know that you are stressed.

2.   Understand the "true" source of your stress.

Often people believe stress is caused by an external situation or person. In truth, people react differently to the same situations, so stress cannot be caused by the situation. Therefore, recognize it is your automatic, inborn, hard-wired reaction to the situation or person that actually causes you to experience the "Fight or Flight" response and its negative physical, mental and emotional effects.

The underlying "hard-wiring" of your mind, as an ENFP or ENTP, predicts that you will automatically react by withdrawing to rehash the past.

When you recognize your signs of stress, you can choose to **STOP** the automatic, hard-wired responses, and take back control of your emotions and behavior. Understanding the true source of your stress gives you the power to choose how to act in the face of stress.

3.   As soon as you recognize you are in your "Stress Mode," STOP and take a few slow, deep breaths.

Breathe in through your nose as if you are breathing air into your stomach and then out through your mouth.

This is called deep breathing, conscious breathing or diaphragmatic breathing. This causes an automatic "Relaxation Response" in your body and your mind, which counteracts the "Fight or Flight" response.

4.   Once you have relaxed your mind and body, consciously "shift" to your "Best Mode" – **EXTRAVERTED INTUITION.**

   ✓   Get out of your head and start talking, even if you are by yourself. You can even talk to yourself in the mirror to better help you figure out everything that is possible!

   ✓   Focus on all that's possible in the future, rather than rehashing the past.

   ✓   Focus on what you can do to make the future even better because of what you've learned from the past.

You got it! You are now in control!

Go to www.Lulu.com and type in "Stress Reduction Guide" to get the Guide for your Type. It includes your driving force, 4 inborn strengths and 4 strategies to reduce your stress and enhance your relationships.

Chapter 16 - ESTJs and ENTJs under Stress

Under stress ESTJs and ENTJs, tend to be flooded with emotion. Why?

Normally both of these Personality Types are guided by their ability to get things done using logic. Their Best Mode of Operating is **Thinking**. They are **Extraverts** who naturally focus on getting results.

ESTJs are focused on projects. As "S"s, they are usually focused on supervising people to complete projects that are similar to ones they have done in the past.

ENTJs are focused on more long-term, strategic projects. As "N"s they enjoy creating a strategy and then marshalling the right people to carry it out.

For ESTJs and ENTJs, emotions are unsettling. They are usually thrown off balance by problems in a relationship. They become inwardly emotional and lose their ability to take decisive action to solve the problem. Why?

When stressed, the body reacts by going into "Fight or Flight." And, the brain shuts down – switching to its most primitive way of operating. There is no time to process things, the brain reasons, there is an emergency, just REACT! The least effective mode of operating for ESTJ and ENTJ is **Feeling** – the opposite of their highly developed **Thinking**. And, because they are Extraverts, their stress is Introverted; they withdraw from the world!

When stressed ESTJs and ENTJs lose track of the logic of the situation that usually grounds them and become overwhelmed by emotion. They feel sad, lonely, angry or hurt.

Sound familiar?

If you are ESTJ or ENTJ (or you know someone who is) what can you do? Follow these steps to return to balance.

Follow these steps to return to balance.

1. Learn to recognize your Stress Mode -- **EXTRAVERTED FEELING**.

    Whenever you notice that you are:

    ✓   Being indecisive.

    ✓   Withdrawing from the world and not feeling like participating.

    ✓   Feeling hurt, unappreciated or frustrated with others.

    ✓   Blaming yourself for problems and losing your "can do" attitude.

STOP and notice that these are just signs that you are stressed; this is not who you are! There is nothing wrong with you; it is simply your mind's way of letting you know that you are stressed.

2. Understand the "true" source of your stress.

    Often people believe stress is caused by an external situation or person. In truth, people *react* differently to the same situations, so it cannot be caused by the situation. Therefore, recognize it is your automatic, inborn, hard-wired *reaction* to the situation or person that actually causes you to experience the "Fight or Flight" response and its negative physical, mental and emotional effects.

    The underlying "hard-wiring" of your mind, as an ESTJ or ENTJ, predicts that you will automatically react by withdrawing to feel emotional.

    When you recognize your signs of stress, you can choose to **STOP** the automatic, hard-wired responses, and take back control of your emotions and behavior.

    Understanding the true source of your stress gives you the power to choose how to act in the face of stress.

3. As soon as you recognize you are in your "Stress Mode," STOP and take a few slow, deep breaths.

    Breathe in through your nose as if you are breathing air into your stomach and then out through your mouth.

    This is called deep breathing, conscious breathing or diaphragmatic breathing. This causes an automatic "Relaxation Response" in your body and your mind, which counteracts the "Fight or Flight" response.

4. Once you have relaxed your mind and body, consciously "shift" to your "Best Mode" - **EXTRAVETED THINKING.**

    ✓ Get out of your head and start talking, even if you are by yourself. Go do something that reminds you of your competence.

    ✓ Rather than thinking about everything that is wrong, focus on the things that are working and a single step you can take toward getting things back on track - even in a troubled relationship.

    ✓ Think about what might be stressing the other person and what you could do to help them.

You got it! You are now in control!

Go to www.Lulu.com and type in "Stress Reduction Guide" to get the Guide for your Type. It includes your driving force, 4 inborn strengths and 4 strategies to reduce your stress and enhance your relationships.

Chapter 17 - ESFJs and ENFJs under Stress

Under stress ESFJs and ENFJs tend to be become critical and picky. Why?

Normally both of these Personality Types are enthusiastically supporting people. Their Best Mode of Operating is *Feeling*. They are *Extraverts* who naturally focus on helping others.

ESFJs are happiest when they are supporting people in a structured and practical way. As "S"s, they are usually focused on doing things in the here-and-now that help those they care about.

ENFJs are happiest when they are teaching others. As "N"s they are focused on solving problems that require their unique ability to see what might work better for someone.

For ESFJs and ENFJs, feeling useless is difficult. They lose their usual ability to be supportive and become negative and critical. They lose their energy and their ability to demonstrate their support for others.

When stressed, the body reacts by going into "Fight or Flight." And, the brain shuts down – switching to its most primitive way of operating. There is no time to process things, the brain reasons, there is an emergency, just REACT! The least effective mode of operating for ESFJ and ENFJ is **Thinking** – the opposite of their highly developed **Feeling**. And, because they are Extraverts, their stress is Introverted; they withdraw, sit and criticize!

When stressed ESFJs and ENFJs lose track of the relationships that are important to them and become negative.

Sound familiar?

If you are ESFJ or ENFJ (or you know someone who is) what can you do? Follow these steps to return to balance.

Follow these steps to return to balance.

1. Learn to recognize your Stress Mode – **INTROVERTED THINKING**.

    Whenever you notice that you are:

    ✓   Withdrawing from the world and not feeling like participating.

    ✓   Being hyper-critical of yourself and others.

    ✓   Focusing on your problems rather than what you can do to help others.

    ✓   Being negative instead of positive about your life and relationships.

STOP and notice that these are just signs that you are stressed; this is not who you are! There is nothing wrong with you; it is simply your mind's way of letting you know that you are stressed.

2.   Understand the "true" source of your stress.

Often people believe stress is caused by an external situation or person. In truth, people *react* differently to the same situations, so it cannot be the situation that causes the stress. Therefore, recognize it is your automatic, inborn, hard-wired *reaction* to the situation or person that actually causes you to experience the "Fight or Flight" response and its negative physical, mental and emotional effects.

The underlying "hard-wiring" of your mind, as an ESFJ or ENFJ, predicts that you will automatically react by withdrawing and focusing on what is wrong in your life.

When you recognize your signs of stress, you can choose to **STOP** the automatic, hard-wired responses, and take back control of your emotions and behavior. Understanding the true source of your stress gives you the power to choose how to act in the face of stress.

3.   As soon as you recognize you are in your "Stress Mode," STOP and take a few slow, deep breaths.

Breathe in through your nose as if you are breathing air into your stomach and then out through your mouth.

This is called deep breathing, conscious breathing or diaphragmatic breathing. This causes an automatic "Relaxation Response" in your body and your mind, which counteracts the "Fight or Flight" response.

4.   Once you have relaxed your mind and body, consciously "shift" to your "Best Mode" - **INTROVERTED THINKING.**

✓   Get out of your head and start talking, even if you are by yourself. Look in the mirror and give yourself the kind of pep talk you often give others!

✓   Rather than thinking about everything that is wrong, focus on the things that you are grateful for!

✓   Go do something that reconnects you with people you care about to remind yourself how much you love supporting something bigger than you!

You got it! You are now in control!

Go to www.Lulu.com and type in "Stress Reduction Guide" to get the Guide for your Type. It includes your driving force, 4 inborn strengths and 4 strategies to reduce your stress and enhance your relationships.

Chapter 18 – Shift From Stressed To Best™

Make the most of yourself, for that is all there is of you.
-- Ralph Waldo Emerson

What You Now Know:

✓ There are 16 inborn Personality Types which define how people interact with the world around them.

✓ You know there are no "good" Types or "bad" Types just <u>individual</u> Types.

✓ You understand your own hard-wired Personality Type and accept that you cannot change it. It's yours - you own it!

✓ You understand that owning your Personality Type gives you the opportunity and the power to choose to be more effective.

✓ You realize that the people in your life also have hard-wired Personality Types and you cannot change them!

✓ You know what causes you stress and how to deal with it.

✓ You realize you can reduce your stress by practicing what you've learned.

✓ You realize you can also improve all of your interpersonal relationships by practicing what you've learned.

This understanding is the first step to reducing the stress in your life as well as improving every relationship in your life.

What To Do Next:

Now it's time to think about everything you've learned and make a personalized action plan to:

✓ Apply what you've learned.

✓ Provide a personal roadmap to follow whenever you face any stressful situation.

✓ Use over and over again anytime you want to improve a relationship.

From Stressed To Best™ Personal Action Plan

My Personality Type is:_____

My Stress Mode is:_____ My Best Mode is: _____

Here Is My Four-Step Program for Shifting *From Stressed To Best*™

1. I will be consciously aware of *my signs of stress*: _____

    _____

    _____

    _____

2. I will then remember that the true source of my stress is my reaction, not the situation, *and I will choose to STOP my automatic reaction.* (Because people react differently to the same situations, it is my personal, individual *reaction* to the situation or person that actually causes the "Fight or Flight" response and its negative physical, mental and emotional effects. The underlying "hard-wiring" of my mind, identified by my Personality Type, predicts the type of stress I will have, and how I will react to it. It is at this point that I can *choose to stop the automatic*, hard-wired responses, and take back control of my emotions and behavior. Understanding the true source of my stress gives me the power to choose how to act in the face of that stress.)

3. To regain control, *I will STOP and take a few slow, deep breaths*. (Breathing in through my nose as if breathing air into my stomach and then out through my mouth. I now know that this deep breathing causes an automatic "Relaxation Response" in my body and my mind to counteract my automatic stress reaction.)

4. Now having relaxed my mind and body, *I will consciously gain control and shift to my Best Mode* by:_____

    _____

    _____

    _____

    _____

You got it! YOU are now in control!

Acknowledgements

We are grateful to the many clients, colleagues and friends for their encouragement and continuing support during the development and refinement of the **From Stressed To Best**™ program. You truly did keep us going by providing the feedback and inspiration we needed along the way!

A special thanks to:

> ***Rudy Platzer*** (INTJ) – The "MASTERMIND of Perfection," for his hard work and expertise in scripting and editing this book. He helped us take it from an idea to a reality!

> ***Renee Konzen*** (ISFJ) – Our "Always Ready HELPER," who so willingly does anything and everything to support us. We are truly appreciative to have had her continuing help over the years!

David would also like to take this opportunity to acknowledge his father, John D. "Jack" Prudhomme, a Navy aviator and Vietnam hero who is listed as MIA. His memory provides him with inspiration each and every day.

About The Authors

Ruth E Schneider (INTP) has a life-long dedication to helping individuals and organizations achieve their goals. With over 25 years of experience as a manager, educator, and consultant she has a diverse combination of knowledge of motivation, personality types, problem solving, team work, productivity, innovation and interpersonal dynamics.

Ruth is a graduate of Eastern Illinois University with a BA in Experimental and Clinical Psychology. She has a MS in Logistics and Organizational Science from the Air Force Institute of Technology. Ruth has also completed Post Graduate work in Executive Coaching from the College of Executive Coaching.

Her experience includes:
- Management of a world-wide USAF aircraft maintenance productivity improvement program, documenting $250M in savings over 5 years.
- Director of Human Resource Development for an organization of 35,000 employees. Managed a staff of 135 trainers and program managers and a $6M annual budget.
- Creator and manager of an internal management consulting organization for a 3-star General and his staff.
- Contract innovation consultant and trainer to government agencies and private corporations.
- Co-founder of two successful small businesses.

She is certified as:
- A Master Innovator.
- An MBTI® Master Practitioner.
- A Stress Reduction Specialist.
- A Diabetes Motivational Coach.
- A Consulting Hypnotist.

Ruth brings this wealth of experience to bear as co-author of *From Stressed to Best.* She looks forward to continued work helping people reduce their stress so they can lead more effective and satisfying lives.

E-mail: Ruth@MederiWellness.com

David S Prudhomme (ENFP) is the Founder and Director of the Mederi Wellness Center.

David brings a unique approach to wellness borne of his life-long quest to understand the mind and body. He has developed an approach to wellness that is powerful, thought-provoking, and well-grounded in the latest research. His contribution is his ability to bring together the latest research from seemingly disparate sources. David expertly integrates the most current research from the sciences of the conscious and subconscious mind, nutrition, philosophy, biology, anthropology, medicine, history, spirituality, brain chemistry, physics, engineering, and Neuro-Linguistic Programming.

His varied experiences and studies led him to establish the Mederi Wellness Center, where he has long been successful in helping people "Shift their lives from where they are to where they want to be" using the power of their mind. Every day he helps people make powerful life changes mentally, physically and emotionally. Clients leave the office inspired and energized. Their lives change that very day as they take back control of their thoughts, emotions and behavior.

David has studied the mind and body with experts all over the world. He holds certifications as an MBTI® Step I™ and Step II™ Practitioner, Stress Reduction Specialist, Wellness Consultant, Consulting Hypnotist and Diabetes Motivational Coach. He is also a Master Practitioner of Neuro-Linguistic Programming.

Prior to founding Mederi Wellness, David was a very successful high-end medical technology sales person to cardiologists, electro-physiologists and cancer pathologists, and an investigative reporter for an ABC Affiliate.

David is a graduate of the United States Naval Academy with a BS in Engineering and served as a Marine Corp Officer and aviator in Desert Storm. He has an MA in Broadcast Journalism from Boston University.

E-mail: David@MederiWellness.com

Learn More About *FROM STRESSED TO BEST*™

Visit our website: www.StressedtoBest.com

Connect with us on Facebook: www.Facebook.com/StressedtoBest

You may find the following companion products and services helpful.

For Self-help: We've developed a full line of self-help products including Stress Reduction Guides and Workbooks by Type to help you go *From Stressed to Best*™.

> *Stress Reduction Guides (one for each Personality Type).*

> *How to Shift From Stressed To Best.*

> *Live and Work in Harmony with All 16 Personality Types.*

For Helping Others: Whether you are a teacher, coach, parent, trainer, helping professional or organizational development practitioner, we offer books and tools for your use in helping individuals, families and teams move *From Stressed to Best*™.

> *Detailed Summaries For All 16 Personality Types.*

> *CLUES: How to Estimate Personality Type through Observation and Conversation.*

> *A Guide To Understanding the Eight Stress Modes.*

> *How To Work Effectively With all 16 Personality Types.*

> *A Guide To Using the MBTI® Step II™ Profile for Targeted Stress Reduction.*

> *Strengths, Stressors and Suggestions Workbook (for each Type).*

> *Complete Interpretive Report for use with the MBTI® Step II™ Profile (for each Type).*

> *Complete Interpretive Report for Understanding all 16 Types for Use with the MBTI® Step II™ Profile.*

For Trainers: Our Training Kits for facilitators include PowerPoint slides with scripts, group and individual exercises, participant action plans and a facilitator copy of the companion participant book. Training Classes include:

- ➤ *How to Shift From Stressed To Best.*

- ➤ *Live and Work in Harmony with all 16 Types.*

- ➤ *Interpreting your MBTI® Step II™ Profile with emphasis on Stress Reduction and Wellness*

The Authors are also available for:

- ➤ Speaking Engagements.

- ➤ Corporate Seminars and Training Programs.

- ➤ Affiliate Program Development.

- ➤ Certification Training Programs.

- ➤ Individual Consultations.

Contact the authors for more information.

www.StressedToBest.com

Ruth E Schneider: Ruth@MederiWellness.com

David S Prudhomme: David@MederiWellness.com